Gooseberry Patch

Cozy Country
CHRISTMAS

W9-CEF-746

A Country Store In Your Mailbox®

Gooseberry Patch
600 London Road
P.O. Box 190
Delaware, OH 43015

www.gooseberrypatch.com
1·800·854·6673

Copyright 2006, Gooseberry Patch 1-931890-89-7
Second Printing, February, 2007

Do you have a tried & true recipe...
tip, craft or memory that you'd like to see featured in a **Gooseberry Patch** book? Visit our website at **www.gooseberrypatch.com**, register and follow the easy steps to submit your favorite family recipe. Or send them to us at:

Gooseberry Patch
Attn: Book Dept.
P.O. Box 190
Delaware, OH 43015

Don't forget to include the number of servings your recipe makes, plus your name, street address, phone number and e-mail address. If we select your recipe, your name will appear right along with it...and you'll receive a **FREE** copy of the book!

Table of
CONTENTS

DEDICATED
to

Our family & friends...may your
Christmas be filled
with cozy country pleasures.

With warmest
APPRECIATION

Thanks to all who shared a favorite
recipe or heartfelt memory with us...we
wish you a merry Christmas and a
sleigh-full of sweet
new memories!

Heartwarming Holiday
MEMORIES

Janie Reed
Gooseberry Patch

The day before Thanksgiving, we invite extended family & friends who will not be spending the actual holiday with us to join together for a day of baking and meal prep. This includes all ages from grandmas to toddlers. We make all our traditional dishes and everyone is welcome to bring a new recipe, as well. We always include some extremely simple ones so the kids can really get involved. There are games and other activities as well as some fluffy pillows and blankets in an adjacent room for little ones to nap. At the end of the day, everyone takes their recipes home with them so they are prepared for the big day. This time spent together creates as many wonderful memories as the holiday itself. Happy holidays!

Julie Garofalo
Farmington, MN

The day after Thanksgiving is a happy, warm day for our family. We crank up the Christmas music, bring out all of our Christmas decorations and our 2 children help decorate the tree. They receive new ornaments to add to their collection. That night we celebrate by turning off all the lights and having a "make your own pizza" party. We spread out a blanket by the Christmas tree and eat by the twinkling lights. Afterwards, we watch a favorite Christmas movie together. Last of all, we start the annual storybook countdown to Christmas. Beforehand, I've wrapped up lots of Christmas-themed books and our kids each get to unwrap one to read before bedtime. This day really gets us in the mood for a great holiday season!

Heartwarming Holiday MEMORIES

Francie Stutzman
Dalton, OH

Growing up in the small town of Shreve, Ohio, I could hardly wait for our dad to say, "It's time to get the Christmas tree!" He'd load us kids into the car to make the trip to the nearby farm, and we'd trudge through the snow to pick out that special tree. After we found it, my dad and brother would carefully cut the tree down. Then we'd hurry home to a warm supper that Mom had prepared, with the expectation of making our tree the most beautiful ever! After Dad had the tree set up, it was time to do the decorating. Boy, did we have fun! We all participated so that the tree was adorned with its beautiful decorations, including old baby rattles. We'd "ooh" and "aah" over it, and just sit and take in the pine scent and the love that surrounded us. Oh, the wonderful memories!

Phyllis Ridenour
Bellflower, CA

Every year on the first Saturday in December, my family has our Christmas progressive dinner. We've done this for 9 years now! We always start at our house with appetizers and proceed on, walking to 10 or more other homes for salads, soups, main dishes and desserts. We all look forward to it…the evening is so much fun! Everyone decorates their homes, plays Christmas carols and prepares wonderful food. Everyone lives nearby as it is like our own little community, but no matter where you live, you can always plan something like this with your neighbors. It's a delightful way to get together and gives everyone a chance to show off their favorite holiday dish.

Janet Allen
Hauser, ID

Christmas was definitely a religious holiday to my mother. Like many families in the 1950's and 1960's, we didn't have a lot of money, but she was determined to have a nice nativity set for our home at Christmas time. I have a heartfelt memory of going to Woolworth's with my mother before Christmas and purchasing a cardboard stable. All the figures were sold separately...luckily, Woolworth's carried these same sets for years. The first year we took home Mary, Joseph and the Baby Jesus to go with our stable. Every year, we trudged through the snow to purchase a few more figures, until my mother felt the set was complete. My mom has been gone for many years now, but 40 years later the cardboard stable has a place of honor in my home at Christmas...along with Baby Jesus, Mary, Joseph, 2 shepherds, 2 angels, 3 wise men, 2 sheep and a camel.

Mary Torrance
Henderson, NV

When our children were little, we lived in Rochester, New York, where cold and snow were always plentiful. We started the yearly tradition of the Christmas light expedition. After dinner on the Sunday before Christmas, the kids take their baths, snuggle into their PJ's and bundle up for our car tour of Christmas lights. We make hot cocoa for our ride and drive around to local neighborhoods and businesses that decorate for Christmas. We've since moved to the southwest and our kids are a bit older, but we still carry on this tradition and reminisce about decorations past. It's a wonderful family tradition for just our family...we are too selfish with this tradition to invite others to share!

Heartwarming Holiday MEMORIES

Kristin Berke
Walnutport, PA

I have many wonderful Christmas memories of growing up in the small town of Northampton, Pennsylvania. My mom would help my brother and me create a Christmas countdown chain. We would hang it on our bedpost and faithfully remove a link each night until the last magical night. On December 6th, Saint Nick always paid us a visit and left treats of apples, oranges, nuts, a gingerbread man and a small toy. Around this time, we would all eagerly aid my dad in putting up the Christmas putz or nativity, complete with trains, houses, tree and people ice skating on a lake. Once Christmas arrived, there was always a feeling of wistfulness, as we knew it would be another year until we could repeat the ever-anticipated Christmas rituals in our household.

Mary Therese Onoshko
Brick, NJ

Every year at Christmas, my children and I make dozens of cookies from recipes we pick out of our many **Gooseberry Patch** cookbooks. We make a special little craft that we have selected from one of the craft books. Then we put them together in special bags and deliver them via wagon throughout the neighborhood. When we started, we had just moved here and didn't know many people at all. Now our list is up to 19 and will be growing for next year. It's a great way for the children to recognize the importance of giving and reaching out to others. We've made a lot of new friends along the way too!

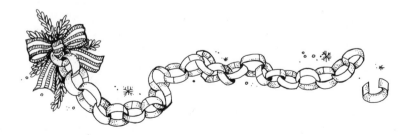

Kathy Daynes
Littleton, CO

Several years ago I purchased a set of Christmas dishes for the holidays. Every Thanksgiving weekend, I bring out the Christmas dishes and put away the everyday dishes. We use the Christmas dishes for all our meals during December. It certainly brings smiles to our faces at every meal! We have Christmas glasses and silverware as well. The Christmas glasses have a holly motif on them with a white goose on each glass. There is one glass that only has the bill and webbed feet of the goose. It has become a game that the person who gets that glass at dinnertime receives an extra dessert. It is so much fun!

Lori Mulhern
Rosemount, MN

This past Christmas, another mother and I organized a Christmas holiday tea for our daughters, their girlfriends and their mothers. The girls had graduated from high school the previous June and were coming home from college for Christmas. We wanted to get them all together for a special holiday gathering. Each girl brought a small gift to exchange and the mothers brought their favorite holiday treats to share. The house was beautifully decorated, we all wore our holiday best, the mood was festive and we had a lovely display of assorted sweets, cider and coffee. The best part, though, was the girls sharing their new experiences as college freshmen and reminiscing about old times, and also for us moms to sit back and be proud of these beautiful young women. The evening was well received by everyone...we look forward to doing this again in Christmases to come.

Heartwarming Holiday MEMORIES

Diane Snyder
Cleveland, TN

When I was a child, on Christmas Eve we always put out empty baskets on the front porch as soon as it got dark. After supper we could check on them. If they were filled with fruit and our favorite snacks, it meant the elves had come by to see if we were good, and Santa would make his stop later. It helped make Christmas Eve so much fun and easier for eager children to get through. We would take our baskets to bed after eating most of the goodies, excited and happy. I did this for my children and now they do it for their children too.

Tammy McKinney
Sparta, TN

When we were kids, money was tight. My mom wanted to make it seem like we were getting a lot for Christmas, even when we really weren't. She would get a big box for each of us 4 little girls and fill them with small, inexpensive things like paper, pencils, erasers, socks, hair barrettes, little toys, all kinds of small items. She stayed up late for a week to wrap every item in comic strip paper. On Christmas morning she would slide a big box in front of each of us, and we opened presents for what seemed like an eternity! We really felt like we were getting lots for Christmas even though Mom didn't have to spend a lot. We loved it. About 20 years later, my sisters and I got together and did the same thing for her…she loved it too!

Jennifer Wood
Gooseberry Patch

Every Christmas, my brother and I got up really early to see what Santa had brought us, while my mother & father were still asleep. I would help my brother down the stairs because he was 4 years younger, and we would go to the stockings. They were always empty, and we would run to Mom & Dad's room with disappointment in our voices. They always told us, "Now, Santa just hasn't made it all the way out here yet! We live WAAAAY out in the country and he hasn't had time to deliver to everyone. His elves called us and said he'll be here soon, if you go back to bed for half an hour." And every year, I would help my brother back up the stairs and we would lie in bed together, whispering about what Santa might have in store for us. We watched the clock carefully and tiptoed downstairs at the appointed time. Sure enough, the stockings would be full! After a few years, I figured it out, but I went along with Mom & Dad's story for a few more years until my brother caught on as well. We still giggle about our little family in our tiny farmhouse, so far out in the country that Santa had to get to us last and if we just went to bed for 30 more minutes, he would be right there!

Luann Barbagallo
Bridgeport, NJ

My favorite memory is of our family lighting bayberry candles early on Christmas Eve. This started way back, probably with my mother's mother, and now I continue this tradition. We NEVER blew them out…they had to burn all the way down by themselves. When I was young, I didn't understand why, when I woke up on Christmas morning, the candlesticks were sitting in the bathtub! Now I fully understand, and I have taken on the task of finding the candles for myself, my daughter, my mom and my niece. To this day, I still love the smell of bayberry at Christmas!

Heartwarming Holiday
MEMORIES

Paula Myers
Tyler, TX

After a lifetime of hectic Christmas mornings, my mother faced her first holiday season alone. The 3 of us daughters knew that first thing in the morning, she would put on a pot of coffee and bring in the newspaper, so we conspired to arrange for her a private visit from Saint Nick. We made a stocking with "Nana," the grandkids' name for her, on the top. All fall we collected special little gifts to fill it. Very late on Christmas Eve, one of us made the trip to her house and hung the stocking on her mailbox. Mother was delighted and baffled! She had no idea who could be responsible. For 19 years we continued to play Santa for her. Early in December we sent a postcard from the North Pole, reminding her to hang her stocking on Christmas Eve. Of course she quizzed each of us, and we continued to deny our involvement. It was the highlight of my holiday every year…listening for hints of things she might like and selecting gifts that wouldn't give me away as the giver, then seeing Mother line up all her treasures to show them off, never knowing who they were from. Giving in secret is very different from the usual giving we do. I can't recommend it enough!

Brenda Degreenia
Barre, VT

I remember the excitement of Christmas shopping at the 5 & 10 cent store. My mother did not have much money in the 1950's but she really made a little go a long way. I remember gathering around the piano with my 2 brothers and my sister to sing while my mother played. We were not the best singers but it gave us all that special feeling of family. Getting up on Christmas morning with the wood stove roaring, the smell of popcorn balls and of course the tree and presents…we had to have breakfast first before we could open the presents. My mom really made Christmas special!

Linda Taylor
Nebo, KY

We live out in the country, across the road from my parents. We celebrate Christmas every year with my aunts, uncles and cousins, who all come to my mother's home. A few years ago, my husband decided to bring out his big amplifier and hook up Christmas music to it. I was the first to arrive home from work that Christmas Eve, and when I got out, the music just filled the air everywhere! As each car drove up and everyone got out, it was wonderful to watch the expressions on their faces. Now it has become a tradition for us. When it snows, it really brings a "White Christmas" home!

Peggy Mayfield
Cedar Park, TX

My mother-in-law collected little elves as her 3 boys grew up. These were always the first of the decorations to come out, and she placed them carefully, peeking out from behind bookends, tucked into a nook, with just the head peeking out. When we started our own family, I began to collect elves too, and now, the weekend after Thanksgiving, the elves begin to appear...at first, only a couple, tucked under the Thanksgiving centerpiece, or behind the cookie jar on the windowsill in the kitchen. Later, as we get closer to Christmas, all the elves appear. When they were very little, our children thought that these were Santa's helpers, coming to check up on them to see if they had been naughty or nice. Now, the older ones help find good "peeking places" that the youngest is sure to see!

Heartwarming Holiday
MEMORIES

Peggy Donnally
Toledo, OH

My early childhood Christmases were amazing! My brothers, sister and I would wake up Christmas morning not only to toys under the tree, but also to the tree itself...a holiday feast for the eyes. My mother would wait to decorate until Christmas Eve, after we were fast asleep. I don't know how she did it! She has since admitted that sometimes she'd just barely climbed into her bed as we were climbing out of ours. I still remember coming downstairs to a tree in front of the window, where the couch had been just hours before. It was lit from top to bottom with big old-fashioned multi-colored glass lights, Shiny Brite ornaments, ropes of sparkling garland and strands of silver icicles. Our red felt stockings with frosty mica Santas were on the mantle, stuffed with tangerines, ribbon candies and candy canes. There were musical Christmas bells, little felt elves, sprigs of mistletoe and a big bowl of nuts topped with a nutcracker. My mother not only made those Christmases magical, she made memories!

Christine Margocs
Austin, TX

My father was in the Army, and we moved around quite a bit while I was growing up. A steadfast Christmas tradition that never changed, however, was getting a REAL Christmas tree each holiday. Our tour of duty in Bangkok, Thailand did not change this...my dad paid extra to have the tree shipped in! In Italy we rented our lodgings, and the owner let us plant the 3 trees we bought, roots and all, each Christmas there. To this day, we get a live tree each holiday. This Christmas, my husband and I took our children to a tree farm to cut our own. Nothing beats the look and smell of a real tree!

Kimberly Lottman
Bedford, VA

A few years ago, when our young daughter first became old enough to understand Santa Claus and Christmas, she was worried that Santa would not be able to leave his presents because we don't have a chimney. Thinking quickly to reassure her, I remembered an old antique key that I had displayed on a shelf in my bedroom. I went and got it, and explained to her that this was Santa's magic key that he used to get into our house on Christmas Eve. She was immediately relieved! Now each year we keep the key hanging on a red ribbon on the front doorknob of our house. It has become one of my favorite traditions since it was born out of the magical faith of a child. I am certain that long after my daughter is grown, we will still be sure to put out Santa's magic key!

Stella Hickman
Gooseberry Patch

Every Christmas, my Dad and Mom and I would bundle up and drive downtown before dark for the big Christmas parade. We'd walk with a gathering crowd to High Street and my dad would perch me on his shoulders so I wouldn't miss a thing. Most important to me was the gentleman on the very last float…I asked my parents over and over, "When will Santa get here?" Dad said to listen for the song "Santa Claus is Coming to Town." Finally, the last band came by and everyone sang along with the band as Santa, his reindeer and sleigh floated high over a snowy mountain on his float yelling to the crowd, "Merry Christmas, everyone!" Around the float marched a crew of little green elves throwing gift bags of candies and funny toys to the kids lining High Street. I believed the "real" Santa had come to Columbus that night and I was going to sit on his lap at Lazarus department store and tell him what I wanted.

Marjorie Nye
Staunton, VA

When my children felt they were a little too old to sit on Santa's lap, but were still reluctant to give up the magic altogether, I thought of a way they could still participate in a way that was comfortable for them. I had each child write a letter to Santa and include their wish list. I slipped the letters into envelopes in which I had placed a few spoonfuls of fireplace crystals, then we all gathered around the fireplace. I told the children to watch carefully as I tossed each letter into the flames. They "ooh'ed" and "aah'ed" as the letters burned and beautiful blue, green and orange flames appeared. I explained to them that the colored flames were really "wish fairies" who were taking their special wishes to Santa Claus. My children are nearly grown now, but fondly remember the wish fairies and plan to carry on the tradition when they have children of their own.

Connie Toussaint
Plano, TX

Every Christmas Eve, in his big rush to deliver presents to all the good boys and girls, Santa accidentally leaves North Pole snow trailing from our fireplace to the tree. Although we're usually half asleep by the time all the gifts are wrapped and under the tree, my husband always remembers to get out his hunting boots and sprinkle baking soda around them to make the tell-tale prints. This year my 8-year-old son even scooped up some "snow" in a baggie to prove Santa's existence to any non-believers at school!

SharonLee Tyler
Swanton, VT

Many years ago when my 2 children, Chris and Tami, were only 6 and 9, they started a tradition on their own that they still follow to this day. They would buy each other a small Christmas gift to be put in their stockings on Christmas Eve, and before they went to bed, they each took their gift out of their stocking. I didn't know they had been doing this until several years had passed and my daughter told me about it. They still continue this tradition today at ages 35 and 38. I have picked up the idea and put a small gift in each of their stockings (as well as the 4 grandchildren's) for them to have on Christmas Eve. It still impresses me to this day that 2 little children would start this tradition!

Faith Deaton
Southaven, MS

My 3 sisters and I always spent Christmas Eve at my grandparents' home. We'd have a special meal, watch Christmas specials on TV and drink eggnog. When it was time to go home, my grandmother would give each of us a new nightgown that she had made for us. We'd put on our nightgowns and go home with Mom & Dad. Back home, we would sit by the Christmas tree while my mom read the story of Jesus' birth and "The Night Before Christmas" (with Dad acting out all the motions). Then we'd say our prayers and go off to bed. It wasn't until years later that I realized the time at my grandparents' home was both a great tradition for my sisters and me, and also gave "Santa's elves" time to finish up their work.

Heartwarming Holiday MEMORIES

Joan Brochu
Hardwick, VT

The Christmas of 1958, I was so lonesome, living 240 miles away from my family. This was always such a big holiday in our lives. When your husband is a farmer, though, it's very hard to get time off. We had been married for 4 years and had a son 2 years old. It was sad to think that my parents would not be with us to celebrate and to watch our son open his gifts. On the Saturday before Christmas, we were watching *Gunsmoke* on TV. They sang a Christmas carol on the show and we sang along. When it was over, the music continued. We thought we were hearing angels...we really did! We looked out the window and lo, and behold! The angels were my mother and dad, my youngest brother Bart and youngest sister Georgianna. I can't even begin to tell you of the tears in our eyes. What a Christmas!

Elizabeth Trythall
Sitka, AK

I have many wonderful, warm Christmas memories, but the one that really stands out in my mind is the year that my father was unemployed. Money was very tight, so my mother checked out thrift stores for gifts for my sister and me. On Christmas morning, I received a beautiful doll bed with new sheets, a pillow and quilt. My doll was freshly scrubbed and her hair was soft and clean with bows and ribbons in it. Mother had found a used doll bed and painted it like new with pretty decals. She sewed the sheets, quilt and doll clothes from scraps she'd gotten from her quilting friend. It was the most beautiful present that I ever remember receiving. I wish I still had that doll and bed! But I believe I played so much with it, that I wore it out.

Linda Mills
Pasadena, MD

One of my most memorable Christmas memories happened when my sister Ruth, my brother Dan and I were only 8, 6 and 4. Dad and Mom had bought us a toy train. It was big, probably 24 inches long. They hid it in the hall closet, wrapped. Well, we got to snooping around one day looking for hidden presents when we opened up the closet. Reaching for something else in the closet, Dan, or it might have been Ruth, stepped on the train. To our horror, it let out a big "WHOOOOOOOOOO" sound!!! We were all so surprised and afraid of getting caught in the act of snooping, that we slammed the closet door shut. I don't think any of us went looking for presents again that Christmas! Of course, there were other Christmases...ha!

Annette Mullan
North Arlington, NJ

I remember on Christmas Eve my mom would stand by the window and shout to my brothers and me, "I see Santa, come quick!" But, of course, by the time we got to the window, he'd already have flown off. She told us this was because "You need to be in bed in order for Santa to deliver your gifts." So up to bed we went...we were so excited! This went on for as long as I can remember. Even when my younger siblings came along, we all did this for them. Now that I'm a grandmother of 2 beautiful small boys, my son has started this with the older one. The look on his face is priceless!

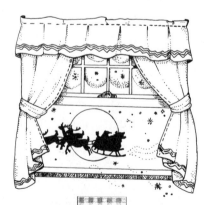

Heartwarming Holiday
MEMORIES

Monica Davis
Wren, OH

My parents were hard-working people with 6 children, and they made sure that we created wonderful Christmas memories as a family. Our grandparents, Vern and Marie Densel, had a getaway cabin in Ontario where we sometimes went for Christmas. It was a long trip with us all squeezed into Dad's station wagon...it seemed like forever until we got there! We would spend 4 or 5 days at their cabin, singing, wrapping gifts and just enjoying our time together. The days started out with snowmobiling, snowman building and sledding. Then we went inside to warm up with some of Grandpa's homemade soup, always served with Grandma's made-from-scratch bread or crescent rolls. Sometimes Grandma used the fireplace to cook large kettles of ham & beans or beef stew. She baked pies and popped corn for us to snack on too. Board games and cards by the fire took up our evenings. Grandpa would make his famous toffee and we set the pan out on the snow to harden. Before we knew it, our brief time with our grandparents would come to an end and it was time to head for home. Now I smile, just thinking back to those special Christmases...they made us feel like the greatest grandchildren alive!

Lindy Acree
Fairbanks, LA

My parents always made my Christmas so special that the memories are abundant. My father would go and cut the top out of a pine tree, then add extra limbs to make it full. We flocked it and brought it inside. The tree was so pretty with the lights! I would lie down in front of the tree with a pillow. Mom and Dad would cover me with one of my grandmother's quilts and let me sleep there all night. It was so special to wake up with all of the lights off and only the Christmas tree lights to see. Thanks to my parents for still making Christmas special after 45 years!

Martha Ober
Oklahoma City, OK

When my husband and I had been married less than 2 years, we were living 250 miles from home with our 6-month-old daughter. We could not afford to go home. On Christmas Eve, my husband came home with a small Christmas tree…it was the most beautiful tree I had ever seen! On Christmas morning we opened the presents we had given to each other and to our daughter. That afternoon, it began to snow, which really made me homesick. Suddenly we heard footsteps coming up our back porch. We looked out and saw a rather large man in boots and an overcoat. He was carrying a large box. When he came to the door, he said that he was from our hometown and knew my parents. They had found out he was coming this way and asked him if he would deliver our Christmas presents from both of our parents! It was almost as fun as if Santa had come to see us. You can imagine how much fun we had digging into that large box and unwrapping all of those presents! I will never forget that Christmas and neither will my husband. We've been married for over 40 years now and it is still fresh in our memories.

Nancy Rhoades
Lebanon, MO

Years ago, we used to attend Christmas Eve services at a small country church. There was always such anticipation in young and old alike that when you walked in, you could feel the spirit. The room was very small and always packed. One year after the Christmas play, the church's pastor invited everyone to stay for refreshments and fellowship. Then he added, "You know, I heard Santa Claus may stop and pay us a visit." Our son Lance, who was almost 3 years old, stood up in the pew and shouted, "No he's not, he's at my house!" Needless to say, we'll never forget that Christmas!

Heartwarming Holiday MEMORIES

Amy Hanna Steiner
Delta, PA

My husband gave me the greatest Christmas present ever! Back in the early 1900's, our 2 families had owned neighboring farms in the small town of Black Horse, Maryland. Fifteen years ago, his family bought the Hanna farm, my family's farm. Todd and I love primitive antiques and rustic farming implements, and I had wanted an antique sleigh for the front porch of our soon-to-be-built home at Christmas time. As it turns out, the Hannas had left their sleigh stored in the rafters of the barn. Todd (who was my fiancé at the time) found out about the sleigh and approached our families about buying it. On Christmas morning of 2002, we had a huge snowstorm and I thought it would take a small miracle to see Todd at all that day. But he made the 15-minute trip to my house in about an hour and picked me up. We proceeded to his family's barn to exchange presents, which I thought was a little odd. He slid the barn doors open, and there it was...my family's sleigh! The paint was beautifully intact in hues of red and black, as was most of the wool upholstery!

I couldn't believe my eyes. Come to find out, Todd's grandmother rode with the Hannas in their sleigh many a time when traveling to church and other activities. Now "our" sleigh sits on the front porch of our new country home, adorned with greens, berries and gifts. It continues to bring us joy every year.

Amanda Homan
Gooseberry Patch

I love getting together for the holidays. My mother-in-law makes the best Christmas dinner! Turkey and gravy, cranberries, pumpkin pie, you name it. My favorite time is after everyone is done eating...we are so full and sleepy that everyone has to take a nap! One year, my husband and I found a spot by the fireplace and curled up together in a recliner with a blanket and went to sleep. It was so sweet that my mother-in-law took a picture. I love that picture to this day!

Florence Unrau
British Columbia, Canada

My cherished Christmas memory is of my mother. Mom loved Christmas and family. One Christmas when she was in her 70's, she disappeared from the family celebration for about 20 minutes. Just when we were wondering where she was, she reappeared, wearing a grandma-type bib apron and a Santa hat, playing "Jingle Bells" on the harmonica and dancing down the hall to the living room where the family was gathered! She had pinned a Canadian 2-dollar bill to her apron for each member of the family. Mom was always so generous with her time and gifts of love, and this was her little extra for each of us. The children and grandchildren still have a special memory of her doing this! Another year she surprised us with a photo of herself sitting on Santa's knee. She was nearly 80 at the time and still loved to have fun. Mom taught us to enjoy the pleasures of little things and especially of family.

Karen Thomas
Princess Anne, MD

One of my favorite Christmas memories happened every Christmas Eve when I was growing up. Mom & Dad always waited until I had gone to bed to put up the Christmas tree and put out all my presents that Santa had brought me. Our stairs that led to the attic were in direct line to my bedroom. Even though I was asleep, when they opened that attic door and the cold air rushed down into my room, I knew that Santa was on his way. I always called it the Christmas smell! To this day, when Mom and I go up into the attic in her house to get the decorations down, when we open the door I always tell her, "There's that Christmas smell that I always look forward to!" That smell brings back so many happy holiday memories for me, especially since Dad is no longer with us. I think I look forward to that aroma even more than to Mom baking her famous cookies!

Heartwarming Holiday MEMORIES

Lynne Gasior
Struthers, OH

When I was 11, there was a park near my home with a creek that froze over in the winter. All my school friends talked about going there to ice skate. I didn't have a pair of skates and I told my mother that was what I wanted for Christmas. She was a single parent and we lived with my grandparents. One Saturday afternoon before Christmas, my grandfather took me shopping with him. We went to several thrift stores and we found a pair of ice skates that fit me. They were worn and shabby looking, but I didn't care. I took them home and cleaned them up, polished them and then I went skating with my friends! I was so excited to have a pair of skates that I didn't even care that they weren't brand new...when I got on the ice, I felt like a star! That was a wonderful Christmas and winter for me. When I was in my 30's, I was reminiscing with my mother about those old ice skates. She said because she wasn't able to buy me new skates that year, my grandfather had offered to take me to get a pair of used ones. I told her that I loved those ice skates and I will never forget him taking me to buy them. A few years later my mother was able to buy me a brand new pair of ice skates, but the old skates that my grandfather bought me that Christmas still hold a special place in my heart.

Donna Burk
North Huntingdon, PA

A few years ago when my children were small and my husband was on disability, I was worried about just how we were going to get Christmas presents for the family. I started making small crafty projects for everyone. I always tried to get something special for my parents, so I started to crochet an afghan for them. Every week I went to the local Ames store and bought a skein or 2 of yarn. Every night I worked a few hours in order to finish before Christmas. On Christmas morning, I had my big afghan all wrapped and we made our big trip to Mom & Dad's. Everyone was exchanging gifts and I felt a little intimidated by what Mom & Dad had received from my sisters and brothers, when I was just handing the 2 of them one package. When my parents opened my gift, they both got teary eyed and said, "We've wanted you to make us an afghan for years...finally we've gotten our wish!" My homemade present was the best! From that year on, they always receive something that I have made personally and I present my gift with pride.

Sophia Graves
Okeechobee, FL

My most favorite Christmas memory was when I was 6 years old. We lived in western North Carolina and my dad decided to go and cut down our tree himself to save money. He and my brother headed off to the tree farm and just as they left, it began to snow. When they returned, the tree was covered in snow, so we left it on the front porch until the snow melted. When we were finally able to bring the tree inside, it took up the whole wall in the living room and was bending at the ceiling! Mom made hot chocolate and crispy cereal treats for us to sip and nibble on while we decorated the tree. That was the most beautiful tree I had ever seen! Though the presents were few that year, the time we spent together decorating that tree was worth more than money could buy. We still laugh about that tree every Christmas. My dad is gone now, but those memories live on.

Heartwarming Holiday MEMORIES

Sheila Furr
LeRoy, NY

We have a special memory from the year that my children, Betsy and Thom, were 4 and 6 years old. On the day after Christmas, my sister arrived at our house holding something covered with snow in her gloved hand. Excited, she said, "Look what I found on your front lawn!" The children and I looked as she carefully brushed off the snow and revealed a beautiful large gold sleigh bell. We were SURE that it came from Santa's sleigh...Thom said, "Maybe it was Rudolph's!" Every Christmas thereafter, "the bell" has had a special place of honor during the holidays. Numerous people have heard the tale, not to mention the countless first-graders that I taught and shared the bell and story with for 27 years after that! All have been sure that the bell, indeed, was Rudolph's!

Katie French
Portland, TX

My most memorable Christmas ever was in 2004. I live in south Texas and for the first time ever, it snowed on Christmas Day!
Keep in mind, it rarely snows here at all. We made the national news! There were 6 inches of snow in my own front yard. Many people down here had never seen snow and it looked like a scene from *It's a Wonderful Life* on my street.
I think the population of our little town doubled with all the snowmen visiting that day. Everyone turned into little children. People were sledding down the streets on surfboards, air mattresses, trash can lids, anything they could find. Of all my Christmas memories, I will have to say that this one as an adult and mother of 3 is the one I will always remember and cherish.

Nancy Beisler
Uniontown, OH

Ever since I was a little girl, my mom would place a dollar bill in the Christmas tree for every family member. These stayed in the tree until New Year's Day, and then Mom would give us each a folded-up dollar to put in our wallet. She said, "Keep it with you and you'll never be without money." Over the years, I've continued this tradition. Now that our daughters are grown with places of their own, they still get the dollar bills and so do their boyfriends. As we put up the tree, the boys remind me to put the dollars in the tree for good luck. Mom & Dad are gone now, but the dollars and good luck are still with us.

Donna Brake
Denver, NC

Our family softens the post-Christmas letdown by having "January Secret Angels." After all of the Christmas decorations are taken down, we draw names. This is the person you are "secret angel" for in the month of January. You surprise them with little things like finding pajamas already warmed and waiting for you, or a little piece of chocolate under your pillow. On January 31, we meet at a restaurant and order dessert for our person. Then we each slide the dessert over to our special person and all unfolds. It is something we all look forward to!

Julianne Riddle
Woodland Hills, CA

My grandmother had 12 children and raised them on a milkman's salary in the 1940's and 1950's. Many of our family traditions come from those lean years. My favorite, which I have passed on to my own children, is that we make ornaments from felt, cut-out wood shapes or flour-and-salt dough. We decorate with paint, glitter, ribbon, sequins and crystal glaze. Each ornament is dated, and each child keeps his or her favorite ornament for our tree. We give the rest as "love gifts" to family & friends. It's really special to unpack these ornaments from years past…I love looking at the changes the years have brought to my "babies." My children love to see the ornaments that their mommy made over 25 years ago, and their grandma made almost 50 years ago! We think it's a nice way to decorate, and an even nicer way to save precious Christmas memories.

Ann Viviano
Saint John, IN

When I was a little girl, my father would always put up a village under our Christmas tree. It was made up of cardboard houses that were painted and sprinkled with glitter. He would take little mirrors and arrange them around the houses as skating ponds decked out with little people skating on them. The most fun was when he took tiny seashells and arranged them as walking paths through the village! While the village was under construction, Mom would bring us cups of hot cocoa and samples of the cookies she was busy baking. I think of this childhood memory every year as I work on setting up the village in my own house for the Christmas season.

Home for the
HOLIDAYS

Andrea Treadwell
Orrington, ME

We decorate our 1826 Cape house for Christmas using rustic "found" materials like pine cones, strips of fabric for garlands, old ice skates and sleigh bells. I began collecting trees (feather trees, pine cone trees, small artificial trees) then we added snowmen, then Santas, then sleds! We set up displays of our own imagination throughout the house. The great room is painted a deep red and we feature trees, pine cones and dried pomegranates on the mantel. The dining room is more formal and there we place gilded fruit, crystal and cherubs on the mantel. Homemade stockings are hung from both mantels. Our living room has the real Christmas tree, baskets of homespun and grapevine balls and the kids' stuffed Christmas animals plus the nativity. Our house is extremely full of the holiday spirit!

Terri Steffes
Jefferson City, MO

I like to use Christmas cards to decorate a tall pencil tree in our house's entryway. I punch a hole in the corner of each card and use either ribbons or pretty ornament holders to hang them. We receive a lot of cards and it always amazes me how no 2 are ever the same! I get a lot of compliments on how pretty the tree looks.

Julie McCreary
Kent, OH

Having just moved into a house with high ceilings, I was looking for something decorative to hang from the chandeliers. I found a wreath idea in a magazine and took it one step further. I took 2 evergreen wreaths (18-inch and 12-inch diameter) and 3 yards of wide red grosgrain ribbon, cut into one-yard lengths. Placing the larger wreath upside-down, I tied one end of each ribbon onto the wreath, equally spaced. Then I tied the other ends to the smaller wreath, again upside-down, equally spaced and leaving about 12 inches of ribbon between the 2 wreaths. I fluffed both wreaths and suspended them from a chandelier by 3 more red ribbons tied to the top wreath. For a finishing touch, I hooked candy canes onto each wreath. Together, the wreaths look like a tiered Christmas tree...a clean, simple country look that's very pleasing.

Sharon Laney
Mogadore, OH

I hang Christmas cookie cutters from my kitchen window in a swag shape. I tie them with narrow burgundy ribbon, starting with long ribbons at each end and gradually shortening the ribbons towards the center. I use a snowman, angel, bear, candy cane, Christmas tree, Santa and star. So easy and so fun!

Home for the
HOLIDAYS

Jennifer Boyd
Minneola, FL

This year I learned to knit, and I found lots of festive yarns available for the holiday season. I decided to knit a pretty garland for our tree. I used large knitting needles and a brilliant red pompom yarn, casting on just a few (3 to 5) stitches and very simply, in garter stitch, knitted several lengths. This formed long, narrow garlands to wrap around the tree. I got lots of compliments on the color it added to the tree! I liked it so much that I ended up knitting myself a scarf of the same yarn.

Suzanna Simpson
Rohrersville, MD

Here's a nice cozy, homespun alternative to traditional silver Christmas tinsel or garland. Take several yards of your favorite checked homespun fabric...2 different ones look great, for example red and dark green. Cut the fabric into 6-inch by 1-inch strips, tie each strip in a simple double knot around a length of twine, and you're ready to wrap your garland around your Christmas tree!

Cathy McKeighan
Helotes, TX

Each year in our neighborhood, we all set out luminarias on the curbs and common areas. On Christmas Eve, everyone assembles their own luminarias of votive candles, white paper bags and sand, and a couple of neighbors are designated to make luminarias for the common areas. At dusk, we put out the luminarias and help each other light them. The street glows with candles…everyone goes walking to see how beautiful and magical it looks with all the Christmas lights and yard decorations. This is the one night of the year that we actually see all of our neighbors! Sometimes we host an open house for our neighbors during their walk up and down the street, with hot buttered rum, cookies and punch for the kids. We have been doing this for the last 7 years…we even get people who drive in to see our neighborhood because they know we do this every year! The luminarias have been successful even in drizzle, wind and rain.

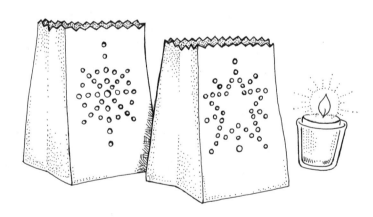

Home for the
HOLIDAYS

Marisa Adams
Manchester, CT

Here's a little something I made quite a few years ago and it just brings so much holiday cheer into my kitchen! I took some cranberry red homespun fabric and made simple curtains to go on my wooden dowel rods. Then I took some green, gold and white fabrics and cut out primitive looking pine trees, snowmen and stars. I fused the cut-outs along the bottom of the curtains, using iron-on fusible webbing. These curtains go up after Thanksgiving and I take them down in early March. They look so colorful and cute...they really take us through the snowy winter months.

Annette Ingram
Grand Rapids, MI

These little bowls, easily made with doilies from a craft store, are charming...a sweet old-fashioned gift when filled with hard candy. Turn a small plastic margarine tub upside-down, cover it with plastic wrap and set aside. Dip a 6-inch doily into liquid fabric stiffener until it's completely wet. Wring out the excess, then lay the doily over the margarine tub. Press it down over the sides, flaring out the edges. Let the doily set overnight to dry, then thread a narrow ribbon through the holes in the doily and tie in a bow. If you like, glue a small Christmas ornament onto the rim of the bowl. Fill with candy and present to a teacher, neighbor or someone else whom you care about!

Susan Stoddart
Newton Falls, OH

I found a childhood photo from back in the 1950's of my husband sitting on Santa's lap, one of myself, same vintage, and one of our daughter in the mid-1980's. I took the 3 photos and placed them in coordinating frames. They make such a nice display for the holidays!

Donna Boulier
White Haven, PA

I have collected many pictures over the years of family members as youngsters posing with Santa. They include my children, their children, a niece and nephews...even one great-grandson! I thought it would be a sentimental idea to display them on our Christmas tree every year with all the other decorations. So I fitted them into plastic key ring picture holders you can get at any craft store or department store, removed the large ring from each and hung them up with ribbons or hooks. It's fun to have people try to guess who is who over the years! This is simple to do and a sweet reminder of days gone by.

Home for the
HOLIDAYS

Danielle Reinhart
Bridgeview, IL

Every year when we are decorating the house for Christmas, my 3 children and I plan a night to sit down and make paper snowflakes. We spend 2 to 3 hours folding and cutting snowflakes together. Then we take thread from my sewing basket and cut 24-inch lengths for hanging to tape to each snowflake. We hang the snowflakes from the ceiling all through the house. It is so neat to see all these flakes moving around with the slightest air movement! Our house is turned into a beautiful winter wonderland…it's a wonderful family tradition.

Jana Scripsick
Sharon, KS

A fond memory that I have at Christmas time from when I was little was making MILES of paper chains for home decor! On the too-cold-to-go-outside days, my mom would keep us busy making chains. Now I have little ones and for this holiday season, we had miles of chains at our house too! Just a lot of colored construction paper and a couple of staplers…the kids love it! We had such a good time making the chains, watching it snow. I never knew how much my mom really appreciated those chains until now. Christmas is so much more special with a little homespun memory!

Diane Floring
Gooseberry Patch

Here is one of my favorite holiday decorating traditions. Each year
I've made my daughter's Halloween costumes. Since there are always
scraps of fabric left over, I make a mini version of the costume (about
4 inches tall) to use as a Christmas ornament. My daughter looks
forward to the ornament as much as the full-size costume. They're
displayed on her own small Christmas tree. She looks forward to
showing the ornaments to visitors, explaining what each costume is
and how old she was when she wore it. We've also added mini
Girl Scout uniforms to the mix.

Kryste Boydstun
Brady, TX

My most special holiday craft is the tree skirts my kids, their daddy
and I have made of red felt. Each year my kids trace their hand and
foot prints around the perimeter of the fabric. I write their name and
the year beside each. Then I adorn it with extra trimmings. It has been
so neat for us to watch as they've grown each year. The tree skirt is
always a topic of conversation for friends and family!

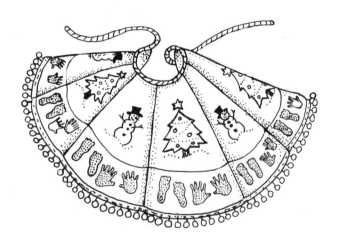

Home for the
HOLIDAYS

Tanya Payzant
Nova Scotia, Canada

Cut hearts, stars or whatever you wish with cookie cutters out of light rye bread. Use a drinking straw to make a hole at the top to insert ribbon once dried, or put a piece of wire through the top to make a loop. Let dry on a tray for several days, turning over each day. When the bread shapes are hard, carefully melt some yummy smelling wax tarts. Dip the shapes several times in the scented, colored wax. Set on a wax paper-lined tray to harden. These fragrant ornaments will last for years!

Kelly Marcum
Dixon, IL

My children and I always make ornaments to attach to our Christmas gifts. This year we tried something completely personalized and totally from the heart. My kids painted their hands with white acrylic craft paint and then wrapped their fingers around a round ball ornament, so the fingers resembled 5 little snowmen. Then we painted on noses and stick arms with a thin paintbrush. We attached this little poem:

> *These are not just 5 snowmen, as anyone can see.*
> *I made them with my little hand, which is a part of me.*
> *So when I'm grown and older, you'll look back and recall*
> *Christmas of 2006…when my hand was just this small!*

The ornaments and poem had my mom, sister and dad in tears! I truly think these are some of the prettiest ornaments on my tree!

Janis Parr
Ontario, Canada

Our feathered friends outdoors need to be remembered during the festive season! I make a garland of pine cones with peanut butter, cranberries, wedges of head lettuce, orange slices and apple cubes. They're simply threaded on fishing line and tied in the tree branches. (Remember to remove the line when the treats have disappeared.) I also make sure to place long, silky strands of hair from my daughter's hairbrush outside in the branches as well. They make a warm, soft nesting material for the birds.

Tori Willis
Champaign, IL

My kids love to make spicy orange pomander balls for the holidays. It's so easy! We get inexpensive jars of whole cloves at a drugstore. Just push cloves carefully through the peel of a whole orange…start with straight lines around the orange, then fill in until it is nearly covered. If the peel is thick, poke holes with a knitting needle, but usually that isn't necessary. Mix up some cinnamon, ginger and nutmeg from the kitchen, a big spoonful of each, and roll the oranges in this mixture. Add some powdered orris root, if you can get it, to help the oranges keep longer. Heaped in a big copper bowl, the pomanders smell so good and look so pretty! Kept in a warm, dry place, they'll dry out slowly and can be enjoyed again next Christmas.

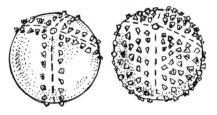

Home for the
HOLIDAYS

Sue Hollenbeck
Vinton, IA

I teach fourth grade and each year all the students get to help decorate the school's tree at Christmas. Each teacher comes up with her own idea for an ornament that the children can make. I live on a farm and we raise cattle so I have an abundance of twine that's been taken off bales of hay. I came up with this idea to make wreaths using the twine. I cut the twine into 12-inch lengths, put 3 lengths together and tape them together at one end. Each child braids the twine…this can be a lesson in itself! Then each braid is formed into a circle, the ends are crossed and hot glued together about one inch from the ends. The children have a choice of colors of very thin ribbon to decorate their wreaths. These look really nice on the tree! Many of the kids ask to make more than one, so they can take one home right away and put on their trees at home!

Laura Kent
Houston, TX

I bought a small rosemary tree for Christmas at a garden store. I wrapped shiny gift paper around the pot, wound wire tinsel garland with stars around the tree and made a looping star of the garland at the top of the tree. Then I clipped on beautiful bird ornaments. I put it in my kitchen and it smelled so good all through the season! In the spring, I planted the rosemary tree in my garden. This would make a great hostess gift too.

Sherry Fisk
Calais, VT

I wanted to share the wonderful Christmas centerpieces we made for our company's Christmas dinner party this year. They were so simple, so inexpensive, and yet created such a Christmasy atmosphere! First we found some beautiful cut-glass type candy dishes in 2 different sizes at a dollar store, then we bought some 5-inch plastic cake-decorating pillars at a craft store. With quick-setting epoxy, we glued one pillar to the inside bottom of each large dish, then glued a small dish to the top of the pillar. I filled the bottom dish with fresh sprigs of cedar and blue spruce, then tucked cinnamon sticks and festive Christmas picks into the greenery. Each small top dish was filled with water, fresh cranberries and a floating candle in various scents and colors. We were very happy with how the centerpieces turned out...with the lights turned down low, our dinner was absolutely gorgeous!

Karen Hruska
Forest, MS

This is a quick & easy centerpiece that looks so pretty! Take a clear glass vase or goldfish bowl and arrange a short string of Christmas twinkle lights inside it. The lights can be either white or multi-colored, just make sure they're safety tested. Run the cord behind the vase, then plug in for a soft, sparkling light. If you like, place a doily over the top and secure it with red, green, silver or gold ribbon. You can also fill the bowl with scented crystals for a scented light.

Home for the
HOLIDAYS

Lynne Gasior
Struthers, OH

I love candles and crafting! When I saw a candle with peppermint candies embedded in the wax, I decided to make my own. Take a bag of peppermints, spray varnish, an ivy bowl or clear glass container, a glass votive cup that's 4 to 5 inches shorter than the ivy bowl, clear gel wax and peppermint candle scent from a craft store. Unwrap the mints, lay them on newspaper and spray with varnish; let dry and spray the other side. When they're dry, arrange mints inside the ivy bowl so centers are facing out. Set the votive cup in the center of the bowl. Following package directions, carefully melt gel wax over hot water in an old saucepan. (Melted wax gets very hot!) Cool slightly, then add scent. Pour wax into the ivy bowl, filling it to within 1/2 inch of the top of the votive cup. When it cools, simply pop in a votive candle and light it. The candlelight glowing through the gel wax is very pretty and the candleholder looks so festive! After the votive candle has burned down, it's easily replaced and you can enjoy your peppermint gel candle over and over again!

Rebecca Varner
Paso Robles, CA

One of my favorite holiday decorating ideas is to drape hollyberry garland with white Christmas lights around the room, in a swag design at the very top of the wall where it meets the ceiling. The lights provide just the right amount of light to create a warm ambience. I like to leave this up until spring comes, when I change it out for a summery ivy garland.

Dana Iungerich
Frisco, TX

This fun little craft is fast to make and so cute! Take a block of wood...I used a 6-inch length of 2x2 pine furring strip. Sand the edges, then lightly brush with white acrylic craft paint. When the paint dries, rub it down with just a little dark shoe polish to give a rustic aged look to your snowman. Now for the fun part, decorating your snowman! Glue on a nose shape selected from a bag of smoker chips and paint it orange. An incense cone could be used instead. Paint 2 dots of black paint for the eyes. A baby sock makes the cap, with the cuff arranged to form the ribbing of the cap. I nailed the sock to the top of the block through the toe, along with a long loop of ribbon for hanging, or you could just glue on the sock. Wrap an 8-inch by 2-inch strip of plaid flannel, cut from one of Dad's old shirts, around the snowman's neck for a scarf and you're done!

Jennifer Sievers
Carol Stream, IL

Here's a decorating idea for the holidays that I enjoy, a display of fresh cranberries and pine for a table top. Take any shape of clear glass vase or bowl...my favorite is a cylinder about 10 inches tall and 4 inches in diameter. I put in a few small pine sprigs trimmed from the Christmas tree, then enough fresh cranberries to fill it about half to two-thirds full. I like to leave some pine sticking out the top of the berries. Once the berries are in, add water to fill the container to about 1/2 inch from the top. Add a tablespoon of bleach to keep the berries from molding. This makes a beautiful decoration, as is, or you can put a floating candle in it for an extra touch! I make several and display them all around my house at Christmas.

Home for the
HOLIDAYS

Debra Altman
Beaufort, SC

I've found a use for all those shiny free demo CD discs that come in the mail...they make a fabulous Christmas wreath! Wrap a 10 to 12-inch styrofoam wreath in festive wide red or green ribbon to cover, hot gluing ribbon at beginning and end. Hot glue discs to flat side of wreath, overlapping them shiny-side up. Decorate the wreath as you like by gluing a small bow in the center of each disc or using acrylic craft paint to dress it up. Attach a picture hanger or wire to the back and voilà...you have a festive wreath. It's a fun project for the kids too!

Ruthann Scott
Capon Bridge, WV

I turn plain clear glass balls from a craft store into really pretty ornaments...it's easy! Remove the metal cap from the ball, then just take squeeze bottles of acrylic craft paint and squeeze a few drops of different colors inside the ball. Spin the ball on a hard surface...if you do this on the floor, it won't drop and break! Spinning will produce a tie-dyed effect. Let the paint dry, then replace the cap. Be creative! You can experiment using a few or many colors.

Lou Ann Genberg
Jamestown, NY

My favorite holiday memory from my childhood in the 1960's was making candy wreaths with my grandmother. She'd bend a wire coat hanger to make it round, leaving the hook on top. We wrapped ribbon round and round, starting at the top, until the circle was completely covered. We'd get many different bags of hard candies. We'd cut little pieces of all different colors of ribbon and use them to tie the cellophane wrapped candies onto the wreath, "smushing" the candies together to make it nice and thick. When the wreath was finished, there were several hundred brightly colored pieces of candy on this edible wreath! My favorites were the cinnamon and nougat candies. Then my grandmother would attach a pair of kids' scissors with ribbon. My brothers and I each got a wreath to take to school for our entire class to enjoy.

Amy Komara
Crystal River, FL

I have a special tablecloth that I use just for Christmas Day. My husband's and my handprints are in the center, with our name "The Komaras" and the year written below them. Around the edges, I started adding our 2 little boys' handprints every year. After they have made their handprints with fabric paints in red or green, I add the year, then sprinkle the handprints with clear, icy glitter before they dry. My boys love doing this and seeing how much they grew since last year! I like to lay a clear plastic tablecloth over it, so that our special tablecloth won't get worn or stained…it is so cute and festive!

Home for the HOLIDAYS

Cheryl Nance
Murfreesboro, TN

We get so many Christmas cards each year from family & friends, and I hate to throw them away! So I thought of a wonderful activity for my 2 kids. When the holiday season rolls around, we spend the day making placemats. The kids make theirs as unique as they are…they each have their very own and oh-so-special placemat for the holidays! They cut out words and pictures and we arrange them like a collage face-down on self-adhesive clear plastic. Sometimes we get really creative with fancy scissors and scraps of holiday paper. After they get the look they want, we cover it with another sheet of clear plastic. We make these for grandparents too. We even make placemats for our pets' food and water bowls. My kids love doing this! They are now 11 and 13 and we've been doing this for 6 years. It gives us some great family time together and it lets them express themselves in their own way.

Susan Huotari
Iron Mountain, MI

Every year I make an advent calendar with old Christmas cards. We cut pictures from the cards into 3-1/2 inch squares and take turns gluing them onto a posterboard calendar that I make and decorate with bits and pieces from the cards. A nativity scene is always saved for the Christmas Day square. I have been doing this since my kids were small. Now they have their own children and neither they, their spouses nor their children can wait to get the new calendar that I make for them each year!

Tina Knotts
Gooseberry Patch

A friend and I had lots of fun getting together to make cookie-cutter felt stars. They're so easy to make, yet look so festive hanging on the tree, on the mantel or even piled in a rustic wooden bowl. To make them, just pin together 2 layers of felt, trace a big star onto the felt and stitch along the outline by machine or by hand. Use pinking shears to cut around the stitching...it can be uneven, that's part of the country charm of these ornaments. Carefully snip a one-inch opening in the back layer only. Push stuffing through the opening until the star is plump, then hand-stitch it closed. We sprayed our stars lightly with spray adhesive and sprinkled them with mica snow and fine glitter. Add a cord for hanging and you're done!

Kerry Hoyle
Pollock Pines, CA

Ever since I became a grandmother, I have made tracings of my grandchildren's hands, The first is when they are born, then I do one before each Christmas. I trace their handprints on wood and cut them out. Then I paint them, including names and dates, to use as ornaments on my Christmas tree. It amazes me how wonderful they all look! My hope is that once the grandchildren are grown, I will pass these ornaments on to them for their own trees. Now that I have 4 grandchildren, the tree is filling up...I may have to have my own special grandbabies' tree soon!

WARM & TOASTY

Christmas Morning Breakfast

Stephanie McAtee
Kansas City, MO

Very early each Christmas, my brother and I always got up quietly to empty our stockings and check out our gifts under the tree. Later Mom would put this breakfast casserole in the oven to bake while we all opened presents. I still carry on this tradition with my own family.

5 slices bread, cubed
1/2 c. shredded Swiss cheese
1/2 c. shredded Cheddar cheese
1/2 c. sliced mushrooms
1-1/4 c. milk

6 eggs, beaten
3/4 c. light cream
1 t. Worcestershire sauce
1 t. dry mustard
salt and pepper to taste

Combine all ingredients in a large mixing bowl; pour into a greased 13"x9" baking pan. Cover and refrigerate overnight. Bake at 350 degrees for 35 to 45 minutes. Makes 6 to 8 servings.

May peace and plenty be the first to lift
the latch on your door,
And happiness be guided to your home
by the candle of Christmas!
-Old Irish Blessing

WARM & TOASTY

Sunny-Side Up Breakfast Egg Pizza

Gladys Kielar
Perrysburg, OH

Delightfully different!

12-inch Italian pizza crust
6 eggs
8 slices bacon, crisply cooked
    and crumbled
1/2 c. red pepper, chopped

1/2 c. green pepper, chopped
1 onion, chopped
1-1/2 c. shredded mozzarella
    cheese

Place pizza crust on a 12" pizza pan. Using a 2-1/2 inch biscuit cutter, cut 6 circles out of crust, evenly spaced and about one inch from the edge. Reserve crust circles for another use. Break an egg into each hole; sprinkle pizza with bacon, peppers, onion and cheese. Bake at 450 degrees for 8 to 10 minutes, until eggs are completely set. Slice into wedges to serve. Makes 6 servings.

Write guests' names on glass balls with a gold paint pen. Set the ornaments in teacups to serve as clever placecards...easy!

Ooey-Gooey Christmas Puffs

Laura Rush
Paso Robles, CA

This is our family's traditional Christmas morning breakfast...it wouldn't be Christmas without it!

8-oz. tube refrigerated
   crescent rolls

8 marshmallows
cinnamon to taste

Unroll crescents and separate into individual triangles. Place one marshmallow at the widest part of each crescent and sprinkle with cinnamon. Roll up dough from long end to short around marshmallow. Tuck bottoms under and pinch to seal tightly. Bake on an aluminum foil-lined baking sheet at 375 degrees for 10 to 15 minutes, or until golden. Place on serving dish and drizzle with icing. Makes 8.

Icing:

1/4 c. powdered sugar

1/4 to 1/2 c. whipping cream

Place powdered sugar in a small bowl. Mix in enough cream to make an icing consistency.

Clip vintage Christmas cards onto pine garland
with red clothespins for a festive
mantel decoration.

WARM & TOASTY

Take & Go Breakfast Cookies

Penny Sherman
Cumming, GA

Perfect for kids who don't want to stop playing with their new toys!

1/2 c. butter, softened
1/2 c. sugar
1 egg
2 T. frozen orange juice
  concentrate, thawed

1 T. orange zest
1-1/4 c. all-purpose flour
1 t. baking powder
1/2 c. wheat & barley cereal

Blend together butter and sugar in a medium bowl until light and fluffy. Beat in egg, orange juice and zest; set aside. Combine flour and baking powder in a small bowl; stir into butter mixture until blended. Stir in cereal. Drop by teaspoonfuls 2 inches apart on an ungreased baking sheet. Bake at 350 degrees for 10 to 12 minutes, until golden around edges. Cool on a wire rack. Makes 1-1/2 dozen.

Decorate plain pillar candles in a jiffy...cut out pictures from Christmas cards and affix with double-sided tape.

Mini Spinach & Bacon Quiches

Vickie

An elegant addition to a holiday brunch buffet.

3 slices bacon, crisply cooked
    and crumbled, drippings
    reserved
1/4 c. onion, diced
10-oz. pkg. frozen chopped
    spinach, thawed and drained
1/8 t. salt

1/2 t. pepper
1/8 t. nutmeg
15-oz. container ricotta cheese
8-oz. pkg. shredded mozzarella
    cheese
1 c. grated Parmesan cheese
3 eggs, beaten

In a skillet over medium heat, cook onion in reserved drippings until tender. Add spinach and seasonings; stir over medium heat about 3 minutes, until liquid evaporates. Remove from heat; stir in bacon and cool. Combine cheeses in a large bowl. Add eggs; stir until well blended. Add cooled spinach mixture; stir until well blended. Divide mixture evenly among 10 lightly greased muffin cups. Bake at 350 degrees for 40 minutes, until filling is set. Let stand 10 minutes; run a thin knife around edges to release. Serve warm. Serves 10.

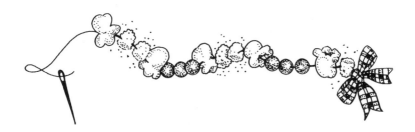

Stringing popcorn is old-fashioned fun! All you need is a big bowl of plain popcorn, a needle and strong thread. Add fresh cranberries or even mini gumdrops for color.

Italian Sausage Frittata

Rosalie Berardo
North Brunswick, NJ

Scrambled eggs with an Italian accent...delicious!

1 lb. ground sweet Italian
    sausage
8 eggs
1/2 c. ricotta cheese

1/2 c. shredded mozzarella
    cheese
1/4 c. grated Parmesan cheese
salt and pepper to taste

Cook sausage in an oven-safe skillet over medium heat until golden;
drain off most of the fat. Whisk remaining ingredients together and
pour over sausage in skillet. Continue to cook over medium heat until
eggs are set, about 5 minutes; do not stir. Place frittata in oven and
bake at 400 degrees for about 10 minutes, or until eggs are golden on
top. Makes 6 servings.

Tie tiny Christmas ornaments onto stemmed glasses
with ribbon bows...so festive for serving orange juice
at a holiday brunch.

Yuletide Coffee Cake

*Sharon Demers
Dolores, CO*

The secret ingredient is cranberry sauce!

1/2 c. butter, softened
1 c. sugar
2 eggs
1 t. almond extract
2 c. all-purpose flour
1 t. baking powder
1 t. baking soda

1/2 t. salt
1 c. sour cream
1 c. whole-berry cranberry
  sauce, divided
1/2 c. chopped walnuts or
  pecans, divided

Blend together butter and sugar; add eggs and extract. Beat until soft and fluffy; set aside. Sift together dry ingredients; add to butter mixture alternately with sour cream. Pour half of batter into a greased Bundt® cake pan. Swirl half of cranberry sauce and half of nuts on top of batter. Add remaining batter, sauce and nuts; spread evenly. Bake at 350 degrees for 55 minutes, or until done. Let cool in pan on a wire rack for about 25 minutes. Invert on wire rack to finish cooling. Turn cake out of pan and drizzle with Almond Glaze. Serves 10 to 12.

Almond Glaze:

3/4 c. powdered sugar
1 T. water

1 t. almond extract

Stir ingredients together
until smooth.

Fill the fireplace with
rows of pillar candles for
a warm, cheerful glow.

Christmas Cranberry-Pecan Loaf

Regina Prince
McCaysville, GA

Top a warm slice with a melting pat of butter...yummy!

1-3/4 c. all-purpose flour
1 c. sugar
1 T. baking powder
1/4 t. salt
2 c. bran & raisin cereal
1 c. milk

1 egg, beaten
1/4 c. oil
1/3 c. orange juice
1 T. orange zest
1 c. cranberries, chopped
1/2 c. chopped pecans

Combine flour, sugar, baking powder and salt; set aside. Mix cereal and milk; let stand 5 minutes. Stir in egg, oil, juice and zest; add to flour mixture until just moistened. Sprinkle in cranberries and pecans; pour into a greased 9"x5" loaf pan. Bake at 350 degrees for one hour and 15 minutes. Makes one loaf.

A generous square of checked homespun makes a
cozy liner for a basket of warm muffins.

No-Fuss Overnight Oatmeal

Lisa Panzino-DiNunzio
Vineland, NJ

Warms you down to your toes!

2 c. long-cooking oats,
   uncooked
3/4 c. raisins
4 c. water

1/8 t. salt
Garnish: maple sugar or
   brown sugar, sliced fruit

Combine oats, raisins, water and salt in a slow cooker sprayed with non-stick vegetable spray. Cook on low setting overnight for 8 to 10 hours. Add sugar to taste; serve with your favorite fruit. Serves 8.

Apple Breakfast Cobbler

Debi Gilpin
Uniontown, PA

What a treat to wake up to on a cold winter morning!

4 apples, cored, peeled
   and sliced
1/4 c. honey

1 t. cinnamon
2 T. butter, melted
2 c. granola cereal

Place apples in a slow cooker sprayed with non-stick vegetable spray. Combine remaining ingredients and sprinkle over apples. Cover and cook on low setting for 7 to 9 hours or on high setting for 3 to 4 hours. Serves 4.

Small drawstring bags sewn of holiday print fabric are sweet table favors. Fill them with packets of flavored tea or coffee for a special surprise.

WARM & TOASTY

Date-Pecan Pancakes

Stacie Mickley
Gooseberry Patch

Stacks of pancakes can be kept warm in a 200-degree oven.

2 c. biscuit baking mix
1/2 t. cinnamon
1 c. milk
2 eggs, beaten

1/2 c. chopped pecans
1/4 c. chopped dates
Garnish: pancake syrup,
   powdered sugar

Stir together baking mix, cinnamon, milk and eggs in a large mixing bowl. Add pecans and dates just until blended. Pour 1/4 cup batter onto a lightly greased griddle; cook until bubbly on surface. Flip and cook until golden on both sides. Garnish with pancake syrup or powdered sugar. Makes 12 pancakes.

Invert a glass garden cloche and fill it with shiny Christmas ornaments, then cover with a plate and turn it right-side up...beautiful!

Ham, Cheddar & Chive Wraps

Jackie Smulski
Lyons, IL

*I love these handy wraps...they're so easy to make and
as yummy as a classic ham & cheese omelet.*

1 T. butter
4 eggs, beaten
1-1/4 c. cooked ham, diced
1/2 c. Cheddar cheese, cubed

2 T. fresh chives, snipped
pepper to taste
4 flour tortillas, warmed

Melt butter in a medium skillet; pour in eggs. Add remaining
ingredients except tortillas. Scramble to desired consistency, until
eggs are set; remove from heat. Place egg mixture in tortillas and
wrap tightly. Secure with toothpicks and serve warm. Makes 4.

Spread out cotton batting as a snowy setting for tiny
vintage houses and reindeer or snowman
figures...what a sweet centerpiece! Add a dash of
mica flakes for icy sparkle.

WARM & TOASTY

Breakfast Logs

Sharon Rogers
Willis, TX

Serve with additional picante sauce on the side.

8-oz. tube refrigerated
   crescent rolls
1 lb. ground pork sausage

1/2 c. cream cheese, cubed
1/2 c. picante sauce

Separate dough into 4 rectangles; set aside. Brown sausage in a skillet; drain. Stir in cream cheese; heat until cream cheese is melted. Stir in picante sauce. Spread sausage mixture across length of each rectangle of dough; roll up. Place rolls on an ungreased baking sheet. Bake at 350 degrees for 9 to 12 minutes, until golden. Makes 4 servings.

Bring farmhouse cheer to the kitchen with a mini Christmas tree...trim it with dried apple and orange slices, sugar cookies hung with ribbons and a big cookie cutter star on top!

Maple Syrup Muffins

Carol Hickman
Kingsport, TN

Pure maple syrup gives the most scrumptious flavor.

1/2 c. milk
2 eggs
3-1/2 c. all-purpose flour
5 t. baking powder
1/2 t. salt
2 c. maple syrup
1/2 c. butter, melted

Whisk milk and eggs together; set aside. Sift together flour, baking powder and salt. Stir into egg mixture alternating with syrup. Stir in butter; fill lightly greased muffin cups 3/4 full. Bake at 325 degrees for 30 minutes. Makes 1-1/2 dozen.

English Muffin Loaves

Carolyn Shonkwiler
Sunbury, OH

Pass the marmalade, please!

5-1/2 c. all-purpose flour,
    divided
2 envs. active dry yeast
1 T. sugar
2 t. salt
1/4 t. baking soda
2 c. milk
1/2 c. water
2 T. cornmeal

Sift together 3 cups flour, yeast, sugar, salt and baking soda; set aside. In a large pot, stir milk and water together over medium heat until temperature is between 120 to 130 degrees. Add flour mixture and beat well; stir in remaining flour to make a stiff batter. Sprinkle greased 8"x4" loaf pans with cornmeal; pour batter into pan. Cover and let rise for 45 minutes. Bake at 400 degrees for 25 minutes; remove loaves from pans. Cool on sides. Serve toasted. Makes 2 loaves.

Overnight Sweet Rolls

Kris Warner
Circleville, OH

This recipe makes 2 pans of sweet rolls...one pan can be frozen before rising, if you like. Later, just remove from the freezer, cover and let rise overnight, then bake in the morning.

3 c. water
1 env. active dry yeast
1 c. sugar
1 T. salt
2 eggs
1/2 c. shortening

10 c. all-purpose flour
1 c. brown sugar, packed
1 c. butter
1-1/4 t. corn syrup
softened butter, brown
   sugar, cinnamon

Heat water until very warm, about 115 degrees. Add yeast and stir to dissolve; let stand for 5 minutes. In a large bowl, stir together yeast mixture, sugar, salt, eggs, shortening and flour; place in a greased bowl. Cover and let rise; punch down once an hour for 5 hours. In a saucepan, melt brown sugar, butter and corn syrup; divide between two, ungreased 13"x9" baking pans. Divide dough into thirds; roll each out to 1/8-inch thick. Spread butter over each; sprinkle with cinnamon and brown sugar to taste. Roll each into a log shape; cut into one-inch pieces. Arrange rolls in pans; cover and let rise overnight. Bake at 350 degrees for 20 minutes. Makes 2 pans, 12 to 15 rolls per pan.

String jingle bells onto lengths of colorful
pipe cleaners and twist the ends
together...fun napkin rings!

Cinnamon Toast

Laura Fuller
Fort Wayne, IN

Grandma always made this for us kids as a treat.

1/4 c. sugar
1 T. cinnamon

5 T. butter, softened
4 slices bread

Combine sugar and cinnamon in a small bowl. Mix butter with one tablespoon sugar mixture. Spread butter mixture on bread; sprinkle with remaining sugar mixture. Broil for 3 to 4 minutes, until crisp and golden. Makes 4 servings.

Mama's Warm Spiced Milk

Loni Ventura
Wimauma, FL

A tummy-warming beverage...tastes like a baked apple in a mug!

2-1/2 c. milk
1/3 c. apple butter
2-1/2 T. maple syrup
1/4 t. cinnamon

1/8 t. ground cloves
Garnish: vanilla powder, 4-inch
  cinnamon sticks

Whisk ingredients except garnish together in a heavy medium saucepan. Heat over low heat until milk steams (do not boil). Serve sprinkled with vanilla powder and a cinnamon stick for stirring. Makes 4 servings.

Add whimsy to an evergreen wreath...tuck in a little bird's nest and a tiny red bird from a craft store.

Almonds & Honey Granola

April Jacobs
Loveland, CO

Serve with icy milk or sprinkle over yogurt as a crunchy topping.

2 c. long-cooking oats,
   uncooked
1/2 c. slivered almonds
1/2 c. sunflower kernels

1/2 c. sweetened flaked coconut
1/2 c. honey
1/2 c. oil
1/4 c. raisins

Mix together oats, almonds, sunflower kernels and coconut in a bowl; set aside. In a separate bowl, mix honey and oil together; pour over oat mixture and stir well. Spread granola onto a greased baking sheet and bake at 300 degrees for 20 to 30 minutes, or until golden. Remove from oven and place in a serving bowl; add raisins. Store in an airtight container. Makes about 4-1/2 cups.

Wrap toss pillows in holiday fabric and tie with
brightly colored ribbons just like gift packages!
Add a few stitches or tiny safety pins to
hold the ribbons in place.

Topsy-Turvy Potato Torte
Jo Ann

Garnish with a sprinkle of chopped chives.

1 c. shredded Cheddar cheese
1/2 lb. bacon, crisply cooked
   and crumbled
2 T. olive oil
3 potatoes, peeled and diced
1/2 c. red pepper, chopped

1/2 c. onion, chopped
2 cloves garlic, chopped
salt and pepper to taste
4 to 6 eggs
1 T. milk

Sprinkle cheese and bacon in an 8" round cake pan sprayed generously with non-stick vegetable spray; set aside. Heat oil in a skillet over medium heat; add potatoes, red pepper, onion and garlic. Cover and cook until potatoes are tender, stirring occasionally. Add salt and pepper to taste. Spoon potato mixture into pan; set aside. Whisk together eggs and milk; add salt and pepper to taste. Pour evenly over potatoes. Bake at 350 degrees for 20 minutes, until eggs are set. Run a knife around edge of pan; invert onto a serving plate. Cut into wedges to serve. Makes 4 servings.

Keep a basket full of Christmas storybooks and
a cozy throw near the fireplace...ready
for a snuggly storytime!

WARM & TOASTY

Slow-Cooker Sausage & Egg Casserole

John Alexander
New Britain, CT

Hearty and filling...enjoy it for dinner on a chilly night!

14 slices bread, quartered
Optional: 2 to 3 T. mustard
1 lb. ground pork sausage,
   browned and drained
2-1/2 c. shredded Cheddar or
   Monterey Jack cheese

1 doz. eggs, beaten
2-1/4 c. milk
1/2 t. salt
1 t. pepper

Spread bread on one side with mustard, if desired. In a greased slow cooker, layer bread, sausage and cheese. Repeat layering, ending with cheese. Beat together eggs, milk, salt and pepper. Pour over ingredients in slow cooker. Cover and cook on low setting for 8 to 10 hours. Makes 6 to 8 servings.

Christmas! The very word brings joy to our hearts.
-Joan Winmill Brown

Mini Sausage Muffins

Jennifer Cole
Covington, GA

Tasty bite-size tidbits...just right for brunch!

1 lb. ground pork sausage,
  browned and drained
10-3/4 oz. can Cheddar
  cheese soup

1/2 c. plus 2 T. water
3 c. biscuit baking mix

Mix all ingredients well. Fill lightly greased mini muffin cups 2/3 full.
Bake at 350 degrees until golden. Makes about 4 dozen.

Brown Sugar Bacon

Melanie Lowe
Dover, DE

Mmm...maybe you'd better double the recipe!

1/2 lb. thick-cut bacon slices,
  cut into thirds

2 T. dark brown sugar, packed

Toss bacon with sugar to coat; arrange on 2 baking sheets lined with
aluminum foil. Bake at 375 degrees until crisp and browned, about
12 to 16 minutes, turning once. Makes 4 servings.

A length of cheerful red
and green plaid fabric is a
quick & easy table runner
for the holidays.

WARM & TOASTY

Cream Cheesy Scrambled Eggs

Marla Raines
San Angelo, TX

Scrumptious with piping-hot biscuits and strawberry jam!

1 lb. bacon or sausage, cut into
    bite-size pieces
10 eggs, beaten

8-oz. pkg. cream cheese, cubed
salt and pepper to taste

Brown bacon or sausage in skillet over medium heat until nearly done; drain well. Lower heat; add eggs, cream cheese, salt and pepper to skillet. Cook and stir until eggs are done. Serves 4 to 6.

Nothing says Christmas like the wonderful fragrance of freshly cut evergreens! Arrange tree trimmings into vases to enjoy the aroma throughout the house.

Caramel Sticky Rolls

Vicki Channer
Fairview Heights, IL

Just as tasty as Mom's caramel rolls...yet oh-so easy to make!

1/2 c. chopped pecans
25-oz. pkg. frozen rolls
3.4-oz. pkg. cook & serve
    butterscotch pudding mix

1/2 c. margarine
1/2 c. brown sugar, packed

Sprinkle nuts in the bottom of a greased 13"x9" baking pan; arrange rolls on top of nuts. Sprinkle dry pudding over rolls; set aside. Bring margarine and brown sugar to a boil together in a small saucepan; pour over rolls. Cover with greased aluminum foil; let rise at room temperature, 6 to 8 hours or overnight. Bake at 350 degrees for 30 minutes. Turn out of pan immediately. Makes about 1-1/2 dozen.

Start a holiday journal...decorate a blank book, then use it to note each year's special moments, meals enjoyed, guests welcomed and gifts given. You'll love looking back on these happy memories!

French Toast Casserole

Lori Hurley
McCordsville, IN

A really simple way to make French toast for a crowd.

1 c. brown sugar, packed
1/2 c. butter
2 c. corn syrup
1 loaf French bread, sliced
   3/4-inch thick

5 eggs
1-1/2 c. milk
1 t. vanilla extract
Garnish: powdered sugar,
   pancake syrup

Melt together brown sugar, butter and corn syrup in a saucepan over low heat; pour into a greased 13"x9" baking pan. Arrange bread slices over mixture and set aside. Mix eggs, milk and vanilla with a whisk; pour over bread, coating all slices. Cover and refrigerate overnight. Uncover and bake at 350 degrees for 30 minutes, or until light golden. Sprinkle with powdered sugar; serve with warm syrup. Makes 6 to 8 servings.

Add big red ribbon bows to stair railings, drawer handles, lamp bases and potted plants for a dash of Christmas color in a snap.

Merry Christmas Morning Bake

Deborah Lindley
Mabelvale, AR

This is always our Christmas morning breakfast...my family loves it!

12 slices bread, cubed
1/2 c. butter, melted
1 lb. ground pork sausage,
   browned and drained

1 doz. eggs, beaten
1-1/4 c. milk
1 c. shredded Cheddar cheese
salt and pepper to taste

Place bread in the bottom of a greased 13"x9" pan; drizzle with butter.
Sprinkle with sausage; set aside. Mix eggs, milk, cheese, salt and
pepper together; pour over bread mixture. Cover; refrigerate overnight.
Bake at 350 degrees for 30 to 35 minutes. Serves 6 to 8.

Sparkly sticks of rock candy are fun
for stirring tea and coffee!

Apple-Pecan Pancakes

Kristine Marumoto
Sandy, UT

Dollop with whipped cream and sprinkle with more chopped pecans for an extra-special breakfast treat.

1 apple, cored, peeled and sliced	1/2 t. salt
1 t. water	1-3/4 c. milk
1 T. brown sugar, packed	2 eggs
2-1/2 c. all-purpose flour	3 T. oil
4 t. baking powder	1/2 t. vanilla extract
1 T. sugar	1 c. chopped pecans

Cook apple with water until slightly softened; sprinkle with brown sugar and set aside. Combine flour, baking powder, sugar and salt; set aside. Beat milk, eggs, oil and vanilla together; stir into flour mixture. Fold in pecans and apples; pour 1/3 cup of batter onto a hot griddle. Cook until bubbles appear on the surface; flip. Cook until golden. Makes 16.

Pile shiny red apples in a rustic wooden bowl for a welcoming centerpiece.

Date-Nut Coffee Cake

Sharon Murray
Lexington Park, MD

*Catch up on the latest news with your best girlfriends over
a pot of spiced tea and this tasty coffee cake!*

1/2 c. shortening	1-1/2 c. all-purpose flour
1/2 c. sugar	1-1/2 t. baking powder
1/2 t. vanilla extract	1/2 t. salt
1 egg	1/2 c. milk

Blend together shortening, sugar and vanilla in a medium bowl. Add egg; blend thoroughly and set aside. Combine flour, baking powder and salt in a small bowl; add to shortening mixture alternately with milk. Spread half of batter in a greased 8"x8" baking pan. Spread with Date Filling; top with remaining batter. Bake at 350 degrees for 45 minutes. Serves 6 to 8.

Date Filling:

1/4 c. butter, melted	1 T. cinnamon
1/2 c. brown sugar, packed	1/4 c. chopped nuts
1 T. all-purpose flour	1/4 c. chopped dates

Combine all ingredients in a saucepan over medium heat. Bring to a boil; simmer just until brown sugar is dissolved and butter is melted.

Turn ho-hum plain kraft paper into ho-ho-ho with holiday rubber stamps and a red or green ink pad...easy enough for a child to do!

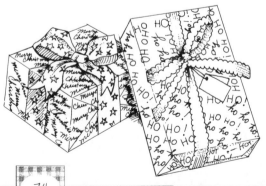

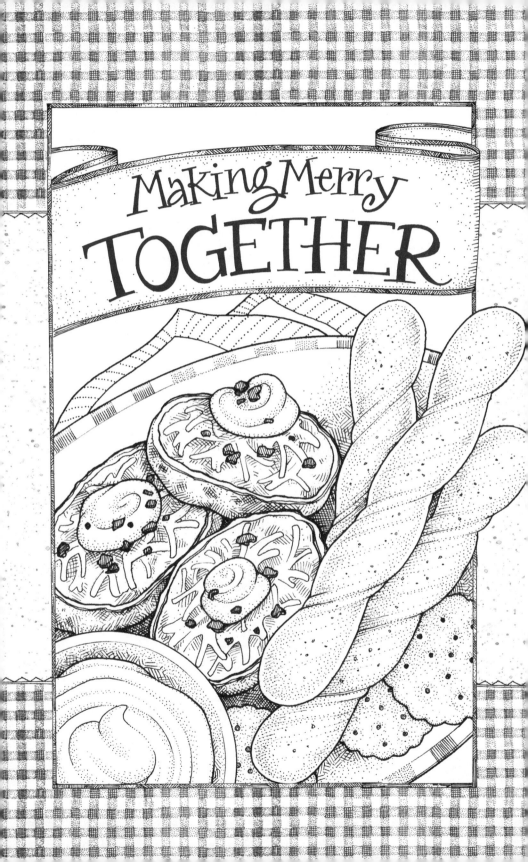

Making Merry
TOGETHER

Tasty White Spinach Pizza

Mike Johnson
Columbus, OH

My own creation...a delicious change from tomato-based pizza.

1 T. garlic, minced
2 T. olive oil
4 c. baby spinach, diced
12-inch Italian pizza crust
1/2 c. Alfredo sauce
1 c. grated Parmesan cheese,
    divided

8-oz. pkg. shredded mozzarella
    cheese, divided
Optional: mushrooms and green
    olives with pimentos, diced

Sauté garlic in oil in a large skillet over medium heat. Add spinach; cook until spinach is wilted and absorbs oil. Remove from heat. Place pizza crust on a lightly greased baking sheet; spread with Alfredo sauce. Sprinkle half the Parmesan and half the mozzarella over sauce. Top with mushrooms and olives, if using. Sprinkle remaining cheese over mushroom layer; top with spinach. Bake at 350 degrees for 15 to 20 minutes, or until golden. Makes 6 servings.

Invite everyone to a tree-trimming party! Lay out a simple buffet of finger foods and put Christmas carols on the stereo...what could be easier or more enjoyable?

Making Merry TOGETHER

Beer-Cheese Fondue

Dale Duncan
Waterloo, IA

Invite some friends over to dip favorite crusty breads in this cheesy hot dip.

10-1/2 oz. can Cheddar cheese
   soup
16-oz. pkg. pasteurized process
   cheese spread, cubed
16-oz. pkg. shredded Swiss
   cheese

1/2 t. hot pepper sauce
2 drops smoke-flavored
   cooking sauce
1-1/2 c. beer or apple cider
bread cubes, fruit cubes
   or slices

Place all ingredients except bread and fruit in a slow cooker; stir to mix. Cover and cook on low setting for 2 hours, stirring after one hour. Whisk to blend. Serve with bread and fruit for dipping. Serves 6.

Black-Eyed Pea Dip

Vickie

Yummy with crispy warm tortilla chips.

16-oz. can black-eyed peas,
   drained, rinsed and divided
3 green onions, chopped
1/2 c. sour cream
1 t. garlic salt

1/2 c. salsa
4 slices bacon, crisply cooked
   and crumbled
tortilla, corn or bagel chips

Set aside 1/3 cup peas. Place remaining peas in a blender; process until smooth. Blend in onions, sour cream and garlic salt. Transfer to a bowl and stir in salsa, bacon and reserved peas. Serve with chips. Serves 8.

Brush pine cones in craft glue, then roll in cinnamon or ground ginger. Heap in a basket for a rustic accent that smells so good!

Walnut-Chicken Spread

Mary Ellen Jernigan
Chesapeake, VA

Perfect for serving at a ladies' luncheon.

1-3/4 c. cooked chicken, finely
    chopped
1 c. walnuts, finely chopped
2/3 c. mayonnaise
1 stalk celery, finely chopped
1 onion, finely chopped
1 t. salt
1/2 t. garlic powder
assorted crackers

Combine all ingredients except crackers; mix well and chill. Serve with crackers. Makes 2-1/2 cups.

Jalapeño Cheese Spread

Kerri Cordova
Martinez, CA

My grandmother used to make this every Christmas.

2 8-oz. pkgs. cream cheese,
    softened
1 t. lemon juice
3 to 4 roasted jalapeño peppers,
    seeded and chopped
2-oz. jar pimentos, drained
    and chopped
1 T. mayonnaise
1/8 t. salt
crackers, tortillas

Mix all ingredients except crackers and tortillas together; refrigerate overnight. Serve with your favorite crackers or on warm tortillas. Makes 2-1/2 cups.

Stack ribbon-tied bundles of sweet-scented candles in a basket near the front door...a pretty decoration that doubles as gifts for surprise visitors.

Mock Champagne

Virginia Watson
Scranton, PA

Serve in unbreakable stemware...the kids can join in toasting!

2/3 c. sugar
2/3 c. water
1 c. grapefruit juice
1/2 c. orange juice
3 T. grenadine
1-ltr. bottle ginger ale, chilled

Combine sugar and water in a saucepan over low heat. Bring to a boil; simmer for 10 minutes. Let cool. Add juices to syrup and chill. At serving time, add grenadine and ginger ale. Serves 6 to 8.

Peppermint Eggnog Punch

Samantha Starks
Madison, WI

Yummy with or without the rum!

1 qt. peppermint ice cream, divided
1 qt. eggnog
4 12-oz. cans ginger ale, chilled
Optional: 1 c. rum
Garnish: 24 mini candy canes

Set aside 2 or 3 scoops ice cream in the freezer for garnish. Soften remaining ice cream; gradually stir in eggnog and rum, if using. Transfer to a punch bowl and pour in ginger ale. Garnish edge of punch bowl with candy canes. Float reserved ice cream scoops on top; serve immediately. Makes 16 servings.

May our house always be too small
to hold all of our friends!
-Traditional New Year's Toast

Hot & Creamy Crab Dip

Teri Lindquist
Gurnee, IL

So rich tasting…serve with baguette slices and crackers.

2 8-oz. pkgs. cream cheese,
   softened
1/2 c. sour cream
1/4 c. mayonnaise
2 T. white wine or chicken broth
2 T. onion, grated
1 T. Dijon mustard

1 t. garlic, minced
hot pepper sauce to taste
6-oz. can crabmeat, drained
1/4 c. fresh parsley, chopped
   and divided
1/2 c. slivered almonds
1/8 t. paprika

Mix the first 8 ingredients together in a saucepan; fold in crabmeat and half the parsley. Cook over low heat until heated through; do not boil. Top with remaining parsley, almonds and paprika. Makes 4 cups.

Corned Beef & Rye Loaf

Janalee Dwojakowski
Schenectady, NY

Always a party favorite.

1-1/3 c. mayonnaise
1-1/3 c. sour cream
1 t. dill weed
2 T. onion, minced

2 T. fresh parsley, finely chopped
2 3-oz. pkgs. deli corned beef,
   chopped
2 round loaves rye bread

Mix together all ingredients except bread. Refrigerate mayonnaise mixture for at least 2 hours. Hollow out one loaf of bread, reserving hollowed portions for dipping; fill with mayonnaise mixture. Cube remaining loaf of bread to use for dipping. Makes about 3-1/2 cups.

Make a fragrant kissing ball…insert
sprigs of fresh rosemary into a foam
ball until covered. Pin on a ribbon
for hanging and top with a fluffy bow.

Greek Spread

Stephanie Doyle
Lincoln University, PA

A must for our parties...guests always request it!

1 c. plus 1 T. chopped almonds,
   divided
8-oz. pkg. feta cheese, crumbled
7-oz. jar sweet roasted peppers,
   drained and chopped
1 clove garlic, chopped

2 8-oz. pkgs. cream cheese,
   softened
10-oz. pkg. frozen spinach,
   thawed and drained
crackers or toasted pita wedges

Line a 2-quart bowl with plastic wrap; sprinkle in one tablespoon almonds. In a separate mixing bowl, mix together 1/2 cup almonds, feta cheese, peppers, garlic, cream cheese and spinach; blend well. Press into bowl over almonds. Cover and chill overnight. Invert onto a serving dish. Remove plastic wrap; press remaining almonds onto the outside. Serve with crackers or pita wedges. Makes about 7 cups.

Odd-shaped gifts are wrapped in a snap...just use fabric! Try red & green dots or a vintage novelty print for fun. Tie with ribbon to match.

Spicy Mixed Nuts

Beth Cavanaugh
Gooseberry Patch

Irresistible for nibbling...makes a welcome holiday gift too.

2 c. dry-roasted peanuts
1-1/2 c. pecan halves
1/4 c. dry-roasted sunflower
   kernels

3 T. roasted garlic vinaigrette
   salad dressing
2 t. ground cumin
2 t. red pepper flakes

Combine nuts and sunflower kernels in a bowl; set aside. Mix together remaining ingredients; pour over nut mixture and toss to coat well. Spread in a single layer on an aluminum foil-lined baking sheet. Bake at 325 degrees for 20 minutes, or until lightly toasted, stirring after 10 minutes. Serve warm or let cool. Makes about 4 cups.

For the easiest-ever tree skirt, simply arrange a length
of brightly colored calico around the
base of the tree.

Zesty Popcorn

Connie Hilty
Pearland, TX

We bet you thought buttered popcorn couldn't get any better!

1/4 c. butter, melted
12 c. hot popped popcorn

.7-oz. pkg. Italian salad
dressing mix

Drizzle butter over popcorn in a large bowl. Sprinkle with salad dressing mix; toss until well coated. Makes 6 servings.

Bacon Bread Sticks

Bonnie Waters
Bloomington, IN

Crispy, crunchy, bacony goodness!

1 c. grated Parmesan cheese
2 t. garlic salt
12 slices bacon, halved

24 4-1/2 inch sesame
bread sticks

Combine Parmesan cheese and garlic salt in a medium bowl; set aside. Wrap each bread stick with a halved slice of bacon, starting at one end and spiraling to other end. Arrange bread sticks on a parchment paper-lined baking sheet. Bake at 350 degrees for 15 minutes, or until bacon is crisp. Remove from oven; immediately roll bread sticks in cheese mixture. Let cool before serving. Makes 2 dozen.

Turn tissue paper into festive filler for gift baskets in a wink...just run it through a paper shredder!

Red & Green Cheese Ball

Gladys Kielar
Perrysburg, OH

Tuck a cheese ball into a pretty basket for a welcome hostess gift.

8-oz. pkg. cream cheese,
   softened
8-oz. pkg. shredded Cheddar
   cheese
2 green onions, chopped

2-oz. jar pimentos, drained
2 T. butter, melted
2 t. Worcestershire sauce
assorted crackers

Beat cream cheese in a mixing bowl until fluffy. Add remaining ingredients except crackers; mix well. Press cheese mixture into a small plastic wrap-lined bowl; smooth top. Cover and chill; remove from refrigerator 15 minutes before serving. Turn out onto a serving plate; peel off plastic wrap. Surround with crackers. Makes one cheese ball.

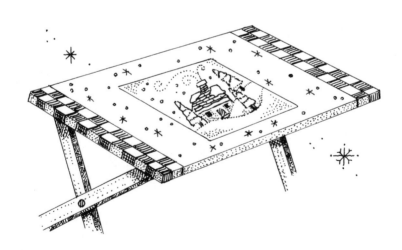

Découpage clippings from holiday giftwrap onto wooden tray tables...so handy when entertaining!

The Cheesy Bowl

Lisa Holdren
Wheeling, WV

My relatives always ask me to bring this warm dip along to family gatherings. I like to serve it in a fragrant loaf of rosemary-olive oil bread from the bakery.

1 c. shredded Parmesan cheese
8-oz. pkg. shredded Colby-Jack
  cheese
2.8-oz. pkg. bacon bits
1 c. mayonnaise

1/2 c. onion, chopped
minced garlic to taste
1 round loaf bread
assorted crackers

Blend together all ingredients except bread and crackers; set aside. Hollow out bread, reserving torn pieces. Spoon dip into bread; place on an ungreased baking sheet. Bake at 350 degrees for one hour. Serve with torn bread and crackers for dipping. Serves 10 to 12.

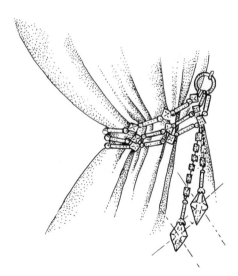

Dress up curtains for the holidays...loop strings of sparkling beads around as festive tie-backs.

Creamy Fruit Dip

Cheryl Grieb
Groveland, FL

A healthy snack for Christmas vacation...use the kids'
favorite flavor of fruit gelatin mix.

8-oz. cream cheese, softened
3-oz. pkg. orange-flavored
   gelatin mix

1/4 c. milk
sliced or cubed fruit

Stir cream cheese in a bowl. Add gelatin mix and milk slowly until
well blended. Chill until serving time; serve with fruit. Serves 4 to 6.

Apple-Walnut Dip

Darla Prizzi
Mentor on the Lake, OH

Yummy with pears too!

8-oz. pkg. cream cheese,
   softened
8-oz. container sour cream
1/4 t. cinnamon
1 apple, cored, peeled
   and shredded

2 T. brown sugar, packed
1/2 c. chopped walnuts
Garnish: cinnamon
apple wedges

Blend together cream cheese, sour cream and cinnamon. Stir in
shredded apple, brown sugar and walnuts; mix well. Chill before
serving. Sprinkle with cinnamon; surround with apple wedges for
dipping. Makes 3-1/2 cups.

Fill a big glass jar with vintage-style
candies...guests of all ages will love
scooping out their favorites!

Hot Buttered Rum

Sue Spann
Murray, KY

Hand out mugs alongside a crackling fire...guests will
be warmed up in no time!

1 c. butter, softened
1 qt. vanilla ice cream, softened
16-oz. pkg. powdered sugar
16-oz. pkg. brown sugar

1 T. cinnamon
1.75-ltr. bottle rum
Optional: nutmeg

Mix together butter and ice cream in a large mixing bowl. Add sugars and cinnamon; blend well with an electric mixer. Freeze in an airtight freezer-safe container. At serving time, scoop one heaping tablespoon ice cream mixture into each mug; add a one-ounce jigger of rum. Fill mug to top with boiling water. Sprinkle with nutmeg, if desired; serve as hot as possible. Makes about 50 servings.

A handmade felt pouch makes a gift card twice as nice!
Use pinking shears to cut 2 small rectangles of red or
green felt, then stitch or glue together on 3 sides.
Decorate with a fun button or charm, or write the
recipient's name with glitter paint...done!

Scrumptious Potato Skins

Nancy Molldrem
Eau Claire, WI

Sprinkle with chopped tomato or green onion for the holidays.

5 Idaho potatoes, baked
1/4 c. margarine
1/4 lb. bacon, crisply cooked
  and crumbled

8-oz. pkg. shredded Cheddar
  cheese
Garnish: 8-oz. container
  sour cream

Cut potatoes in half; scoop out centers of potatoes, leaving a 1/4-inch thick shell. Melt margarine in a heavy skillet over medium-high heat. Add potato centers and cook until golden. Remove from heat; stir in bacon and cheese. Fill potato halves with potato mixture. Serve with sour cream. Makes 10 servings.

Donna's Party Punch

Linda Day
Wall, NJ

This recipe is from a dear friend...it is so easy and tastes so good!

46-oz. can red fruit punch
1 qt. raspberry sherbet, softened

1-ltr. bottle ginger ale, chilled

Mix punch and sherbet together; chill. Add ginger ale at serving time. Serves 10 to 12.

Brighten a green wreath by inserting
sprigs of red berries from a craft store.

Making Merry
TOGETHER

Pepperoni Pizza Twists

Michelle Moulder
The Woodlands, TX

My 2 boys love these!

2 T. grated Parmesan cheese
1/4 t. garlic powder
1/2 t. Italian seasoning
10.6-oz. tube refrigerated
    bread sticks

8-oz. pkg. pepperoni slices
14-oz. jar pizza sauce, warmed

Combine Parmesan cheese, garlic powder and seasoning in a small bowl; set aside. Unroll and separate bread stick dough. Place 2 to 3 pepperoni slices on lower half of each bread stick; fold top half over and twist bread stick. Sprinkle with cheese mixture and arrange on an ungreased baking sheet. Bake at 350 degrees for 12 to 14 minutes, until golden. Serve with pizza sauce for dipping. Makes 10 sticks.

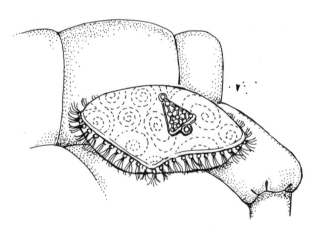

Just for fun, show off Mom's favorite vintage Christmas tree brooches! Pin them onto a velvet cushion and tuck into the corner of the sofa.

Monterey Jack Salsa

Elizabeth Chadwick
Rocky Face, GA

*A deliciously different salsa...surround with
white and red tortilla chips for dipping.*

1 to 3 tomatoes, chopped
4 green onions, chopped
4-oz. can chopped green chiles
2-1/4 oz. can sliced black
    olives, drained
1/4 c. fresh cilantro, chopped

1/2 c. Italian salad dressing
juice of 1 lemon
juice of 1 lime
8-oz. pkg. shredded
    Monterey Jack cheese

Blend all ingredients except cheese together; chill. Stir in cheese at
serving time. Makes 5 to 6 cups.

Bacon & Cheddar Dip

Lecia Stevenson
Timberville, VA

*Crunchy bread sticks and scoop-style corn chips are just right
for scooping up this hearty dip.*

16-oz. container sour cream
1-oz. pkg. ranch salad
    dressing mix

1/2 c. shredded Cheddar cheese
1/4 c. bacon bits

Mix together sour cream and dressing mix; add cheese and bacon bits.
Stir well; chill for one hour before serving. Makes about 2-1/2 cups.

Add pizazz to an appetizer tray...glue tiny Christmas
balls onto long toothpicks for serving.

Mexican Roll-Ups

Joanne McDonald
British Columbia, Canada

Insert colorful party picks before slicing.

8-oz. pkg. cream cheese,
  softened
1 c. cooked chicken, chopped
1 c. shredded Monterey Jack
  cheese
1/3 c. red pepper, chopped

1/4 c. fresh cilantro, chopped
2 T. jalapeño, chopped
2 t. ground cumin
4 10-inch flour tortillas
Garnish: salsa, sour cream

Combine all ingredients except tortillas and garnish; spread evenly over tortillas. Roll up; place on a greased baking sheet. Bake at 350 degrees for 12 to 15 minutes; cut into 1/2-inch slices. Serve with salsa and sour cream. Serves 10 to 12.

Chestnuts roasting on an open fire...scrumptious!
Cut an X in shells with a paring knife to make shelling
easier. Place nuts in a long-handled popcorn popper
and shake over hot coals for about 20 minutes.
Peel and enjoy!

Asian Gingered Shrimp

Lynn Williams
Muncie, IN

Serve with steamed rice for a delicious main dish.

1-1/2 lbs. cooked medium
   shrimp, peeled and cleaned
1/4 c. soy sauce
2 t. fresh ginger, peeled
   and finely chopped
1/4 c. white vinegar

2 T. sugar
2 T. sweet sake or apple juice
1-1/2 t. salt
2 to 3 T. green onion,
   thinly sliced

Arrange shrimp in a single layer in a shallow glass container; set aside. Heat soy sauce to boiling in a small saucepan; add ginger. Reduce heat; simmer 5 minutes, or until most of liquid is absorbed. Stir in vinegar, sugar, sake or apple juice and salt; pour over shrimp. Cover with plastic wrap; refrigerate for 2 hours to overnight. Remove shrimp from marinade with slotted spoon; arrange on serving plate. Sprinkle with green onion. Makes 8 to 10 servings.

Tie ornaments onto the Christmas tree with narrow strips of homespun fabric...sweet and simple!

Making Merry TOGETHER

Shrimp Dip

Jolene Daniels
Alliance, OH

Garnish this dip with a pretend sprig of holly...use mini cookie cutters to cut holly leaves and berries from green and red peppers.

8-oz. pkg. cream cheese,
  softened
1/2 c. mayonnaise
1/2 c. onion, finely chopped

1/2 c. celery, finely chopped
1-1/2 t. lemon juice
1/2 t. Worcestershire sauce
6-oz. can tiny shrimp, drained

Mix all ingredients together. Chill for at least one hour before serving. Makes about 3 cups.

A fragrant, spicy table accent...press whole cloves into the surface of a pillar candle to form a pattern.

Cheery Cherry Cheese Ball

Judy Davis
Bicknell, IN

Keep this yummy treat on hand for impromptu parties!
Simply wrap the cream cheese ball in plastic wrap and freeze.
Thaw at room temperature before serving.

8-oz. pkg. cream cheese,
   softened
8-oz. container frozen whipped
   topping, thawed

1/2 c. powdered sugar
16-oz. can cherry pie filling
graham or wheat crackers

Mix together cream cheese, whipped topping and powdered sugar.
Form into a ball; chill at least 2 hours. At serving time, place cheese
ball on a serving plate; spoon pie filling over ball. Serve with graham
or wheat crackers. Makes one cheese ball.

Slip a packet of spiced tea into a Christmas card to a
dear friend…she can enjoy a hot cup of tea while
reading the latest news from you.

Peppermint Apple Dip

Diann Guy
Tulsa, OK

A quick trick...place candy canes in a heavy-duty plastic zipping bag and crush with a rolling pin.

4 large candy canes, finely
    crushed
12-oz. container frozen
    whipped topping, thawed

Optional: several drops
    red food coloring
apple wedges

Blend crushed candy canes into whipped topping. Add food coloring, if desired. Chill for 2 hours. Serve with apple wedges. Makes about 4 cups.

Remembrance, like a candle, burns
brightest at Christmastime.
-Charles Dickens

Golden North Pole Nuggets

*Betty Stone
Denton, TX*

A sweet & salty treat that can't be beat!

10-oz. pkg. peanut butter chips	1-1/2 c. thin pretzel sticks,
2 T. shortening	broken
6-oz. pkg. plain fish-shaped	
crackers	

Combine chips and shortening in a microwave-safe bowl; heat
on high setting for 2-1/2 minutes. Remove from microwave; stir in
crackers and pretzels. Drop by tablespoonfuls onto wax paper;
let stand 30 minutes. Makes 2 dozen.

Pack up some homemade treats for a yummy gift. Fill a
paper sack, fold down the top, punch 2 holes and
insert a colorful ribbon to tie in a bow. Simple!

Snowdrift Snack Mix

Beverly Vest
Franklin, TN

Send guests home with mini cellophane bags of
this crunchy mix, tied with curling ribbon.

4 c. doughnut-shaped oat cereal
3 c. bite-size crispy corn cereal
   squares
4 c. mini pretzels

2 c. peanuts
16-oz. pkg. white melting
   chocolate, chopped

Mix first 4 ingredients together in a large mixing bowl; set aside.
Melt chocolate in a microwave-safe dish on medium setting for about
2 minutes, stirring once. Pour chocolate over cereal mixture; stir
quickly. Spread mix onto wax paper. After chocolate sets, break apart.
Store in an airtight container. Makes about 13 cups.

Paper baking cups are perfect for serving up party-size
scoops of nuts or snack mix.

Winter Wassail

Linda Cuellar
Riverside, CA

My friend Sandy gave me this recipe when we were caroling together. It was the best wassail I had ever had...it tastes and smells wonderful!

2 c. cranberry juice cocktail
7 c. water
2/3 c. sugar
2 4-inch cinnamon sticks
1 T. whole cloves
1 T. whole allspice

46-oz. can pineapple juice
12-oz. can frozen red fruit
   punch concentrate
6-oz. container frozen orange
   juice concentrate, divided

Combine cranberry juice, water and sugar in a saucepan over medium heat. Tie spices in cheesecloth; add to cranberry mixture. Simmer for 20 minutes. Remove from heat; remove and discard spice bag. Stir in pineapple juice, punch and half of orange juice, using remaining half for another purpose. Heat through; serve warm. Makes one gallon.

Nestle a punch bowl in an evergreen wreath...tuck in fresh red carnations on picks as an accent. So pretty and sweet smelling too!

A FAMILY FEAST

Mmm... So Good!

Maple-Glazed Turkey Breast

Eleanor Paternoster
Bridgeport, CT

*Sprinkle in some sweetened, dried cranberries for an
extra burst of color and flavor.*

6-oz. pkg. long-grain and
   wild rice mix, uncooked
1-1/4 c. water
1-lb. turkey breast

1/4 c. maple syrup
1/2 c. chopped walnuts
1/2 t. cinnamon

Mix together rice, seasoning packet from rice mix and water in a slow
cooker. Place turkey breast, skin-side up, on rice mixture. Drizzle with
syrup; sprinkle with walnuts and cinnamon. Cover and cook on low
setting 4 to 5 hours, or until juices run clear when turkey breast is
pierced with a fork. Serves 4.

Fresh red roses or carnations make a delightfully
different winter centerpiece. Arrange in a big vase
with glossy green holly or delicate ferns.

Perfect Prime Rib Roast

Paula Smith
Ottawa, IL

For special dinners, this recipe never lets me down!

1/4 c. Worcestershire sauce
2 t. garlic powder
2 t. seasoned salt

2 t. pepper
6-lb. bone-in beef rib roast

In a small bowl, combine all ingredients except roast. Rub mixture all over roast; place in a large plastic zipping bag. Refrigerate 8 hours or overnight, turning often. Place roast fat-side up in a lightly greased large roasting pan; pour mixture from bag over roast. Cover with aluminum foil; bake at 350 degrees for 1-1/2 hours. Uncover and bake for an additional 1-1/2 hours, or until roast reaches desired temperature on a meat thermometer, between 150 and 160 degrees for medium. Let stand for 15 minutes before slicing. Serves 6 to 8.

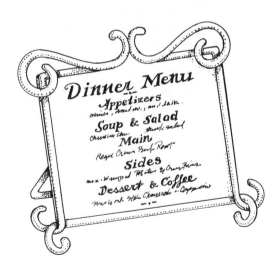

Write out the menu for a special holiday meal and place in an elegant frame...dinner guests will be looking forward to each delicious dish!

3-Cheese Shells Florentine

Sheila Gwaltney
Johnson City, TN

Pass the Parmesan, please!

10-oz. pkg. frozen chopped
   spinach, thawed and drained
1-3/4 c. cottage cheese
1 egg, beaten
1/4 c. grated Parmesan cheese
1 c. shredded mozzarella cheese,
   divided

1/3 c. fresh parsley, chopped
salt and pepper to taste
7-oz. pkg. small shell macaroni,
   cooked
1-1/2 to 2 16-oz. jars Alfredo
   sauce, divided

Combine spinach, cottage cheese, egg, Parmesan cheese, 2/3 cup
mozzarella, parsley, salt and pepper in a large mixing bowl. Set
aside. In another bowl, toss macaroni with 2-1/2 cups Alfredo sauce.
Arrange half of macaroni in a lightly greased 13"x9" baking pan.
Layer spinach mixture evenly over macaroni. Cover with remaining
macaroni, Alfredo sauce, Parmesan and mozzarella, in that order.
Bake at 350 degrees for 35 to 40 minutes. Serves 6.

Put stemmed glasses to use as candle holders...simply
turn them over, placing a shiny ornament ball
underneath. Top each with a short pillar candle.
Group several together on a tray for a table decoration
that's done in a snap.

Pizza Hot Dish

Janet Burr
Juniata, NE

This yummy dish will satisfy the heartiest appetites after an afternoon of sledding and ice skating.

1 lb. ground beef
1/4 c. green pepper, chopped
1/4 c. onion, chopped
20-oz. jar pizza sauce
1/2 t. onion salt
1/4 t. pepper
7-oz. pkg. rotini pasta, cooked

7-oz. can sliced mushrooms, drained
2-oz. can sliced black olives, drained
1 c. shredded Cheddar cheese
1 c. shredded mozzarella cheese

Sauté ground beef, pepper and onion in a skillet over medium heat until beef is browned. Drain. Add pizza sauce and seasonings; simmer for 15 minutes. Spread cooked pasta in a greased 13"x9" baking pan; pour sauce mixture over pasta. Spread mushrooms and olives over top; sprinkle with cheeses. Cover and bake at 350 degrees for 35 minutes. Uncover and bake an additional 10 minutes. Makes 4 to 6 servings.

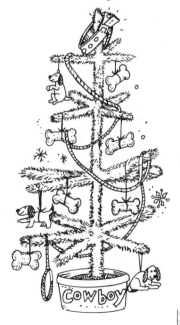

Remember pets at Christmas…they're family too! Trim a whimsical Christmas wreath with kitten figurines, tiny catnip mice and strands of yarn or puppy figurines, dog treats and garlands of leash webbing.

Chicken Chestnut Casserole

Nancy Molldrem
Eau Claire, WI

A great make-ahead dish...pure comfort food.

6 boneless, skinless chicken
   breasts
1 t. salt
8-oz. can sliced water chestnuts,
   drained
2 10-3/4 oz. cans cream of
   mushroom soup

12-oz. pkg. shredded Cheddar
   cheese
2-oz. jar pimentos, drained
1 c. milk
7-oz. pkg. elbow macaroni,
   uncooked
1 onion, finely chopped

Cover chicken with water in a medium saucepan; bring to a boil over medium-high heat. Add salt and simmer until chicken is tender. Drain, reserving 1-1/2 cups broth. Cube chicken; set aside. Mix remaining ingredients and reserved broth in a large bowl. Fold in chicken and spread mixture in a lightly greased 13"x9" baking pan. Cover and refrigerate for at least 12 hours. Bake at 325 degrees for one hour and 15 minutes. Cut into squares and serve. Serves 8 to 10.

Lighted candles on the mantel will glow more brightly
with mirror tiles tucked behind them.

A FAMILY FEAST

Slow-Cooker Beef Stroganoff

Jacque Zehner
Modesto, CA

*A scrumptious dinner that cooks all by itself while
you trim the tree, shop or just take it easy!*

2 T. all-purpose flour
1/2 t. garlic powder
1/2 t. pepper
1/4 t. paprika
1/4 t. dried oregano
1/4 t. dried thyme
1/4 t. dried basil
1-3/4 lbs. boneless beef
   round steak, cubed
10-3/4 oz. can cream of
   mushroom soup

1/2 c. red wine or beef broth
1-oz. pkg. onion-mushroom
   soup mix
8-oz. pkg. sliced mushrooms
1/2 c. sour cream
egg noodles, prepared
2 T. butter, softened
Optional: fresh minced parsley,
   poppy seed

Combine flour and seasonings in a slow cooker. Place meat on top;
toss to coat. Add mushroom soup, wine or broth and soup mix;
stir until blended. Add mushrooms and stir. Cover and cook on high
setting for 3 to 3-1/2 hours or on low setting for 6 to 7 hours, until
meat is tender. Stir in sour cream; cover and cook until heated
through. Serve over noodles tossed with butter; sprinkle with parsley
and poppy seed, if desired. Serves 6.

Ring out a holiday greeting to visitors…hang a string
of sleigh bells on the front door.

Hearty Winter Pork Stew

Jennie Gist
Gooseberry Patch

*Nutritious and filling! Try other varieties of winter squash
too...they're all delicious!*

1-1/2 lbs. boneless pork loin, cubed
2 c. parsnips, peeled and sliced
1-1/2 c. carrots, peeled and sliced
1-1/2 c. butternut squash, cubed

1/2 c. onion, chopped
4 c. chicken broth
1/2 t. salt
1/2 t. pepper
3 T. all-purpose flour
3 T. butter, softened

Layer pork and vegetables in a slow cooker. Top with broth, salt and pepper; cover and cook on low setting for 6 to 7 hours. Blend together flour and butter in a small bowl; gently stir into stew one tablespoon at a time. Raise setting to high; cover and cook for an additional 30 to 45 minutes until thickened, stirring occasionally. Serves 4 to 6.

Now Christmas comes, 'tis fit that we
Should feast and sing and merry be.
-Virginia Almanack, 1766

A FAMILY FEAST

Country Pork & Sauerkraut

Sharon Crider
Lebanon, MO

We eat pork and sauerkraut for luck on New Year's Day...but any chilly day is lucky when this is on the dinner table!

1 T. oil
2 lbs. country-style pork ribs,
    sliced into 4 portions
1 onion, chopped
14-oz. can sauerkraut

1 c. applesauce
2 T. brown sugar, packed
2 t. caraway seed
1 t. garlic powder
1/2 t. pepper

Heat oil in a Dutch oven over medium heat. Add ribs and onion; cook until meat is brown and onion is tender. Combine remaining ingredients and pour over ribs. Cover Dutch oven and bake at 350 degrees for 1-1/2 to 2 hours, until ribs are tender. Makes 4 servings.

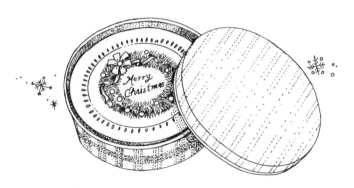

Pick up one or 2 table settings of a different holiday pattern each year. Before long, you'll have a collection of delightfully mismatched dishes and special memories to go with each!

Zesty Italian Pot Roast

Laura Dossantos
Rutherfordton, NC

Just add a loaf of warm bread...dinner is ready!

4 potatoes, peeled and quartered
2 c. baby carrots
1 stalk celery, cut into
   1-inch slices
2-1/2 lb. boneless beef
   chuck roast

1/2 t. pepper
10-3/4 oz. can tomato with
   roasted garlic & herb soup
1/2 c. water
Optional: 1/4 c. all-purpose
   flour, 1/2 c. cold water

Arrange vegetables in a slow cooker. Top with roast; sprinkle with pepper. Mix soup and water; pour over roast. Cover and cook on low setting for 10 to 12 hours. Serve roast surrounded with vegetables; pass drippings in a gravy boat. If a thicker gravy is desired, remove roast from slow cooker; keep warm. Mix flour and cold water; stir into drippings in slow cooker. Turn heat to high setting; cook until mixture boils and thickens, about 10 minutes. Serves 4.

A deep shadow box is a perfect way to enjoy fragile vintage ornaments. Line the inside of the box with gift wrap or cut-outs from Christmas cards.

Chicken & Stuffing Bake

Gina McClenning
Valrico, FL

Herbed stuffing, veggies, raisins, pecans...what a delightful combination of flavors!

4 skinless, boneless chicken
   breasts
salt and pepper to taste
3 T. olive oil
1 onion, chopped
1 c. sliced mushrooms
3 cloves garlic, pressed
10-3/4 oz. can cream of
   mushroom soup
16-oz. container sour cream

1 c. frozen mixed vegetables,
   thawed
1/2 c. frozen peas, thawed
1 c. roasted red pepper, chopped
8-oz. pkg. herb-flavored
   stuffing mix
1/2 c. golden raisins
1/2 c. chopped pecans
1/4 c. butter, melted
1 c. chicken broth

Sprinkle chicken with salt and pepper; set aside. Heat oil in a large skillet over medium heat; add chicken, onion and mushrooms. Cook until golden. Add garlic and sauté for one minute; remove from heat. Cut chicken into bite-size pieces; place in a bowl with sautéed vegetables. Stir in soup, sour cream, mixed vegetables, peas and roasted pepper; pour into a greased 2-quart casserole dish. Combine stuffing mix, raisins, pecans, butter and broth; spread evenly over chicken mixture. Bake at 350 degrees for 45 minutes. Serves 6 to 8.

Turn Christmas cards into festive napkin rings. Cut them into strips with decorative-edge scissors, join ends with craft glue and add a sprig of faux holly...simple!

Beef in Rosemary-Mushroom Sauce

Sharon Demers
Dolores, CO

Add some roasted new potatoes and a simple tossed salad
for an oh-so-elegant yet easy dinner!

1-lb. boneless top sirloin steak,
    about 3/4-inch thick
8-oz. pkg. sliced mushrooms
1 c. white wine or chicken broth
1/4 c. fresh parsley, chopped
    and divided

1 c. green onion, chopped
1-1/2 t. fresh rosemary, chopped
1-1/2 t. balsamic vinegar
4 cloves garlic, minced
10-1/2 oz. can beef broth
8-oz. can tomato sauce

Place steak in a large plastic zipping bag; top with mushrooms and
wine or broth. Refrigerate for 30 minutes, turning occasionally.
Remove steak from bag, reserving mushrooms and marinade. Lightly
spray a large non-stick skillet with non-stick vegetable spray and
place over medium-high heat. Add steak and cook for 6 minutes,
or to desired doneness, turning after 3 minutes. Remove steak from
skillet; keep warm. Combine 2 tablespoons parsley and remaining
ingredients in a medium bowl. Add parsley mixture, mushrooms and
marinade to skillet; bring to a boil. Cook until reduced to 2 cups, about
15 minutes, stirring frequently. Thinly slice steak diagonally across
the grain and place on a serving platter. Spoon sauce over steak;
sprinkle with remaining parsley. Makes 4 servings.

Cover a grapevine wreath with fresh herbs like sage,
rosemary and thyme...simply slip long stems into the
wreath until it's covered. Hang it in a warm place.
The herbs will dry slowly and can be kept for
year 'round decor.

A FAMILY FEAST

Pork Tenderloin & Mustard Sauce

Barbara Schwenk
Muncy, PA

Make the Mustard Sauce a day ahead so the flavors can blend.

1/4 c. soy sauce	2 T. brown sugar, packed
1/4 c. bourbon or sherry	2 1 to 1-1/2 lb. pork tenderloins

Combine first 3 ingredients; pour over pork. Cover and refrigerate for at least 2 hours, turning occasionally. Remove pork from marinade; place in a roasting pan. Bake at 350 degrees for 1-1/2 hours. Serve with Mustard Sauce. Serves 4 to 6.

Mustard Sauce:

2/3 c. sour cream	2 T. dry mustard
2/3 c. mayonnaise-type salad dressing	3 to 4 green onions, chopped

Mix all ingredients together; chill.

Dress up a 3-tiered cake stand in a twinkling...simply fasten tinsel garland around the edge of each tier with double-sided tape.

Tex-Mex Meatball Subs

Tammy Rowe
Bellevue, OH

Serve in paper napkin-lined baskets with chips and a pickle...perfect fare while you're watching your favorite holiday special on TV!

1-1/2 lbs. ground beef
1 egg, beaten
1 c. tortilla chips, crushed
16-oz. jar salsa, divided
26-oz. jar spaghetti sauce

8 hoagie or sub buns, split
1 c. shredded Monterey Jack
  cheese
Optional: jalapeño peppers

Mix together ground beef, egg, chips and one cup salsa. Form mixture into one-inch balls; place in an ungreased 13"x9" baking pan. Bake at 375 degrees for 45 minutes; remove from oven and drain. Combine spaghetti sauce and remaining salsa in a saucepan; heat through and pour over meatballs. Spoon meatballs onto buns and top with cheese. Garnish with jalapeño peppers, if desired. Makes 8 subs.

Gather everyone for a fireside meal...so cozy on a snowy day! Cook hot dogs on long forks or use pie irons to make pocket pies. You can even roast foil-wrapped potatoes in the coals. Let the kids make s'mores for a sweet ending.

A FAMILY FEAST

Slow-Cooker Chicken Tacolados

Wendy Leonard
Travis AFB, CA

Set out bowls of shredded cheese, sour cream, chopped green onions and black olives for guests to add as they like.

5 boneless, skinless
    chicken thighs
2 boneless, skinless
    chicken breasts
10-oz. can green enchilada
    sauce

10-3/4 oz. can cream of
    chicken soup
12 to 15 10-inch flour tortillas,
    warmed
Garnish: salsa

Arrange chicken pieces in a slow cooker; set aside. Combine sauce and soup in a bowl; blend well and pour over chicken. Cover and cook on low setting for 8 hours or on high setting for 4 hours. When chicken is tender, shred with 2 forks. Serve on warmed tortillas; garnish as desired. Serves 6 to 8.

Roll paper doilies into cones and fill with dried flowers for delightful nosegays to tuck among the branches of the Christmas tree.

Bowties with Chicken & Cranberries

Angela Murphy
Tempe, AZ

Try orange or cherry-flavored dried cranberries too!

3/4 c. sweetened, dried
   cranberries
1/3 c. port wine or cranberry
   juice cocktail
1/2 c. shallots, sliced
2 T. butter
1/4 c. all-purpose flour
1 t. paprika

1 t. dried thyme
1/2 t. salt
1/2 t. pepper
1-1/2 lbs. boneless, skinless
   chicken breasts, cut into
   1-1/2 inch pieces
10-1/2 oz. can chicken broth
12-oz. pkg. bowtie pasta, cooked

Combine cranberries and juice in a microwave-safe bowl; microwave on high setting for one minute. Set aside. In a large skillet over medium heat, sauté shallots in butter for 5 minutes. Mix flour, paprika, thyme, salt and pepper in a plastic zipping bag; add chicken and shake to coat. Add chicken and any remaining flour mixture to skillet; cook for 5 minutes. Add broth; simmer for 5 to 6 minutes, stirring occasionally. Drain cranberries; stir into skillet and heat through. Combine bowties with chicken mixture; toss well. Serves 6.

A mini tree decorated with tiny
toys and prizes will delight young
visitors! Let them each choose
one as a take-home gift.

Mustard Short Ribs

Jo Ann

Hearty beef ribs glazed in a savory blend of flavors.

3 to 4 lbs. beef short ribs
1 t. whole cloves
1 t. whole allspice
1 bay leaf
1/3 c. vinegar
1/4 c. honey

2 T. dry mustard
1/2 t. garlic salt
1/2 t. dried tarragon
1/4 t. onion powder
1/8 t. pepper

Place short ribs in a large Dutch oven; add cloves, allspice, bay leaf and enough water to cover ribs. Bring to a boil; reduce heat and simmer, covered, 1-1/2 to 2 hours or until ribs are just tender. Drain; discard bay leaf. For glaze, combine remaining ingredients in a small saucepan. Bring to a boil; reduce heat and simmer, uncovered, for 5 minutes, stirring to blend. Remove from heat. Place ribs in a broiler pan; brush with glaze. Broil, 4 to 5 inches from heat, for 10 to 15 minutes, or until browned, turning and brushing often with glaze. Serves 4 to 6.

Set up a giftwrap station for carefree wrapping. Gather pretty paper, stickers, gift bags and tissue along with scissors, tape and a pen. Just for fun, make a sign for the door that reads, "Please Knock...Elves at Work!"

Beef Burgundy

Virginia Sawdy
Ellenton, FL

Fix & forget!

2 lbs. beef stew meat, cubed
1-1/2 oz. pkg. onion soup mix
10-3/4 oz. can golden
    mushroom soup
4-oz. can sliced mushrooms,
    drained

1/4 c. Burgundy wine or
    beef broth
egg noodles, cooked

Combine all ingredients except noodles in an ungreased 2-quart casserole dish with lid. Cover first with aluminum foil, then the lid. Bake at 325 degrees for about 2 hours. Serve over prepared noodles. Makes 4 to 6 servings.

A basket of pine cone fire starters is a special gift! Carefully melt paraffin or old candle ends in a double boiler and use tongs to dip pine cones. Sprinkle with a little glitter if you like, then set on wax paper to dry.

A FAMILY FEAST

Oven-Roasted Chicken & Potatoes

Karen Mihok
Valencia, CA

*This tried & true recipe is from my 87-year-old
mother...4 generations have enjoyed it!*

4-lb. chicken	1/2 c. boiling water
1/2 t. salt	2 onions, quartered
1/4 t. pepper	12 redskin potatoes
3 T. butter	1 t. dried basil
3 T. olive oil	2 T. fresh parsley, chopped
1 t. chicken bouillon granules	

Sprinkle inside of chicken with salt and pepper; set aside. Melt butter
and oil over medium heat in a Dutch oven. Add chicken and brown on
all sides; remove from heat. Dissolve bouillon in boiling water; add to
Dutch oven. Arrange onions and potatoes around chicken; sprinkle
with basil and additional salt to taste, if desired. Cover and bake at
350 degrees for 1-1/2 hours, basting occasionally with pan juices.
Remove from oven; cut chicken into serving-size pieces. Arrange
chicken on a serving platter with onions and potatoes. Top with pan
juices. Sprinkle with fresh parsley just before serving. Serves 6 to 8.

Make it easy on yourself when planning holiday
dinners...stick to tried & true recipes! You'll find your
guests are just as happy with simple comfort foods as
with the most elegant gourmet meal.

Cajun Pork Sandwiches

Christina Melendez
Lincoln Park, MI

*Prepare in a slow cooker if you like...cook on low setting for
8 to 10 hours or high setting for 4 to 5 hours.*

3 to 4 lbs. pork tenderloin
1/4 c. Cajun seasoning

3 c. water
6 to 8 hoagie or sub buns, split

Combine pork, seasoning and water in a large pot. Simmer for 2 hours over medium-low heat. Remove pork from pot; shred with 2 forks. Spoon meat onto buns and serve warm. Makes 6 to 8 sandwiches.

Make a neighborly gesture...deliver a small
decorated tree and a plate of cookies to an
acquaintance who can't get out easily.

A FAMILY FEAST

3-Cheese Pizza

Stephanie Mayer
Portsmouth, VA

Set out pizza toppings and let everyone make their own!

12-inch Italian pizza crust
2/3 c. pizza sauce
1/2 c. grated Parmesan cheese
1/2 c. shredded Cheddar cheese
1 c. shredded mozzarella cheese

Place pizza crust on a 12" ungreased baking sheet. Spread pizza sauce on top of crust. Sprinkle cheeses over sauce in given order. Bake at 450 degrees for 12 to 15 minutes. Serves 6 to 8.

Slow-Cooker Lasagna

Maria Benedict
Stowe, PA

Use a mixture of ground beef and ground Italian sausage if you like.

1 lb. ground beef
1 onion, chopped
2 cloves garlic, minced
29-oz. can tomato sauce
6-oz. can tomato paste
1 c. water
1 t. salt
1 t. dried oregano
16-oz. pkg. shredded mozzarella cheese
12-oz. container cottage cheese
1/2 c. grated Parmesan cheese
8-oz. pkg. lasagna, uncooked

Brown beef, onion and garlic in a large skillet; drain. Add tomato sauce, tomato paste, water, salt and oregano; set aside. In a medium bowl, stir together cheeses. Layer ingredients in a slow cooker starting with the meat sauce, uncooked lasagna strips broken to fit slow cooker and cheese mixture. Repeat layers twice; finish with meat sauce. Cover and cook on low setting for 4 to 5 hours. Serves 6 to 8.

Tuck a string of tiny white lights into a flower arrangement for extra sparkle.

MMM... So Good!

Cranberry-Glazed Ham

Jessie Gassaway
Zanesville, OH

A glorious baked ham...everyone's favorite!

5-lb. fully-cooked ham
2 to 3 oranges, sliced
1/4 c. whole cloves
1/2 c. cranberry juice cocktail

1/2 c. brown sugar, packed
2 T. honey
1/2 t. dry mustard
1/4 t. nutmeg

Place ham in a roasting pan. Secure orange slices on ham with toothpicks; press cloves into ham surface. Bake at 325 degrees for one hour. Blend remaining ingredients in a small bowl; brush over ham. Bake an additional 40 minutes; let stand for 15 to 20 minutes before slicing. Makes 12 to 16 servings.

March Mason jar luminarias along your front walk.
Simply fill canning jars half full with rock salt and
nestle tea lights in the salt. The flames will make the
rock salt sparkle like ice crystals!

A FAMILY FEAST

Slow-Cooker Chicken & Apples

Janice Woods
Northern Cambria, PA

Serve with baked sweet potatoes...yummy!

6-oz. can frozen orange juice
   concentrate, thawed
1/2 t. dried marjoram
1/8 t. nutmeg
1 onion, chopped
2 cloves garlic, minced

6 boneless, skinless
   chicken breasts
3 Granny Smith apples,
   cored and sliced
1/4 c. water
2 T. cornstarch

Combine orange juice concentrate, marjoram and nutmeg in a small bowl. Place onion and garlic in slow cooker. Dip each chicken breast into orange juice mixture; place on top of onion. Pour any remaining orange juice mixture over chicken. Cover and cook on low setting for 6 to 7 hours, until chicken is almost cooked. Add apples and cook an additional hour, until apples are tender and chicken is thoroughly cooked. Mix together water and cornstarch in a small bowl; stir into chicken mixture. Cover and cook on high setting until sauce is thick and bubbly, about 20 to 30 minutes. Serve sauce over chicken and apples. Makes 6 servings.

Winter is the time for comfort, for good food and
warmth, for the touch of a friendly hand and
for a talk by the fire...it is the time for home.
-Dame Edith Sitwell

MMM... So Good!

Shrimply Spaghetti

Sherry Dominguez
Houston, TX

*I got this scrumptious quick & easy recipe from a
co-worker when I worked in New Orleans.*

1/2 c. butter
1 onion, chopped
1 clove garlic, minced
1 t. dried parsley
1 t. dried thyme
1/2 t. cayenne pepper
1 lb. raw medium shrimp,
   peeled and cleaned

salt and pepper to taste
8-oz. pkg. pasteurized process
   cheese spread, cubed
Optional: milk
spaghetti, cooked

Melt butter in a skillet; add onion and garlic. Sauté over medium heat
until onion is soft. Stir in parsley, thyme and cayenne; add shrimp
and cook over low heat until light pink, about 20 minutes. Season to
taste with salt and pepper; add cheese. Stir until melted, adding a little
milk if desired, to thin sauce. Serve over prepared spaghetti.
Makes 4 servings.

A dish filled with whole
walnuts, almonds and
hazelnuts is a treat for
visitors. Don't forget
the nutcracker!

Linguine & White Clam Sauce

Kristie Rigo
Friedens, PA

Sometimes I add a teaspoon of red pepper flakes along with the oregano...my family likes a little kick!

2 6-1/2 oz. cans minced clams,
    drained and juice reserved
milk
1/2 c. onion, finely chopped
1 clove garlic, minced
2 T. butter
1/4 c. all-purpose flour

1/2 t. dried oregano
1/2 t. salt
1/4 t. pepper
1/4 c. sherry or chicken broth
2 T. dried parsley
8-oz. pkg. linguine, cooked
1/2 c. grated Parmesan cheese

Combine reserved clam juice with enough milk to equal 2 cups liquid; set aside. In a medium saucepan, cook onion and garlic in butter over medium heat until tender and golden; stir in flour. Add clam juice mixture to saucepan; stir until smooth over low heat. Add oregano, salt and pepper; cook until thick and bubbly, stirring frequently. Stir in clams and sherry or broth; cook for an additional minute. Sprinkle with parsley; stir. Toss with cooked linguine; sprinkle with Parmesan cheese. Serves 4.

Spread red or green aquarium sand in a tray
and arrange pillar candles on top for an
easy centerpiece.

Slow-Cooker Potatoes & Ham

Diane Cohen
Kennesaw, GA

Really warms you on a chilly day!

5 potatoes, peeled and sliced
1/2 lb. cooked ham, diced
1/4 lb. pasteurized process
    cheese spread, diced

1/4 c. onion, diced
10-3/4 oz. cream of
    chicken soup

Layer potatoes, ham, cheese and onion in a slow cooker; top with soup. Cover and cook on low setting for 6 to 8 hours. Serves 5 to 6.

Old-fashioned and charming...stencil snowflakes on the windows with glass window wax. After the holidays, just rub off wax with a soft cloth for crystal-clear windows.

Best-Ever Baked Chicken

Sherry Gordon
Arlington Heights, IL

Creamy chicken that's good enough for company.

6 boneless, skinless
   chicken breasts
16-oz. container sour cream

2 c. corn flake cereal, crushed
1 t. Italian seasoning
6 T. butter, melted

Generously coat both sides of chicken breasts with sour cream.
Place corn flake crumbs in a shallow bowl; mix in Italian seasoning.
Dip the sour cream-coated chicken into crumbs. Place chicken in a
lightly greased 13"x9" baking pan. Drizzle with melted butter and
bake at 350 degrees for one hour. Serves 6.

Be sure to set aside one night during the holiday
season to snuggle up with loved ones and watch
favorite Christmas movies!

Reuben Casserole

Mary Ann Nemecek
Springfield, IL

A clever way to make yummy Reubens for the whole gang!

16-oz. pkg. sauerkraut, drained
    and rinsed
1 c. Thousand Island salad
    dressing
1-1/2 lbs. deli corned beef,
    thinly sliced

12-oz. pkg. shredded Swiss
    cheese
4 to 6 slices marble rye bread,
    buttered

Combine sauerkraut and salad dressing; spread in a greased
13"x9" baking pan. Top with corned beef slices evenly placed; sprinkle
with cheese. Place bread butter-side up on top; use enough bread to
cover top, even if it's necessary to cut extra pieces. Bake, uncovered,
at 375 degrees for 25 to 30 minutes. Serves 6 to 8.

A warm country welcome for visitors! Decorate a sisal
door mat using stencils and acrylic paints from a craft
store...try a simple greeting and a holly border. When
the paint is dry, add a protective coat of spray varnish.

Amazing Meatloaf

Staci Allen
Sheboygan, WI

Just like Grandma used to make!

1-1/2 lbs. ground beef
1/2 c. milk
1 egg, beaten
1 T. Worcestershire sauce
1/2 c. brown sugar, packed
1-1/4 c. dry bread crumbs

3/4 c. barbecue sauce
1/3 c. onion, chopped
1 clove garlic, pressed
1-1/2 t. seasoned salt
1/2 t. dry mustard
1/2 t. pepper

Mix all ingredients; spread in a lightly greased 9"x5" loaf pan. Bake, uncovered, at 350 degrees for about 1-1/2 hours. Makes 6 servings.

Hide a small wrapped gift in the Christmas tree for each member of the family to find when putting away the ornaments.

Cheesy Chicken Enchiladas

Andrea Matthews
Lynden, WA

I've been making this dish since college…it's not only a family favorite but is also popular at potlucks.

8-oz. pkg. shredded Monterey
    Jack cheese, divided
1 c. shredded Cheddar cheese,
    divided
3 boneless, skinless chicken
    breasts, cooked and chopped

2 cloves garlic, minced
2 t. chili powder
1-1/2 c. salsa
1-3/4 c. sour cream
10 8-inch flour tortillas

Set aside 1/4 cup of each cheese. Mix remaining cheeses and other ingredients except tortillas. Spoon 1/3 cup mixture into center of each tortilla. Roll up tortillas and arrange in a lightly greased 13"x9" baking pan. Top with remaining mixture and reserved cheese. Bake for 25 minutes at 350 degrees. Serves 6 to 8.

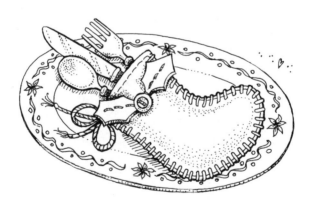

Slip each guest's flatware into a small red felt stocking
and lay on dinner plates for a festive table!

Fireside
FAVORITES

Comfort Chicken Soup

Jenna Albert
Hatboro, PA

Warm & cozy...grandmotherly goodness in a cup!

8 c. water
8 cubes chicken bouillon
6-1/2 c. wide egg noodles,
   uncooked
2 10-3/4 oz. cans cream of
   chicken soup

3 c. cooked chicken, cubed
8-oz. container sour cream
Garnish: dried parsley to taste

Bring water and bouillon to a boil in a large soup pot over medium-high heat. Add noodles and simmer, uncovered, for 10 minutes. Stir in soup and chicken; heat through. Remove soup pot from heat; add sour cream. Sprinkle with parsley to taste. Serves 4 to 6.

Make time for your town's special holiday events. Whether it's a Christmas parade with brass bands, Santa arriving by horse-drawn wagon or a tree lighting ceremony downtown, hometown traditions make the best memories!

Parmesan Crostini

Michelle Sheridan
Gooseberry Patch

Add a dash of garlic powder and thyme for a different taste.

1 baguette loaf, sliced into
   12 rounds

1 to 2 T. olive oil
1/4 c. grated Parmesan cheese

Brush baguette slices lightly with olive oil. Arrange slices on an ungreased baking sheet; sprinkle one teaspoon cheese on each. Place baking sheet under broiler, about 6 inches from heat, for one to 2 minutes, until cheese begins to melt. Makes one dozen.

Look for whimsical giftwrap in unexpected places! Road maps and brown kraft paper are wonderful for wrapping those oversized gifts, while sheets of scrapbooking and origami paper are just the right size for smaller gifts.

Apple-Mallow Yam Bake

Sherry Bell
Palmyra, PA

This family favorite brings back fond memories of my dad,
who really enjoyed it.

2 apples, cored and sliced
1/3 c. chopped pecans
1/2 c. brown sugar, packed
1/2 t. cinnamon

2 17-oz. cans sweet potatoes,
   drained and sliced
1/4 c. margarine, diced
2 c. mini marshmallows

Toss apples and nuts with brown sugar and cinnamon. Alternate layers of apple mixture and sweet potatoes in a greased 1-1/2 quart casserole dish; dot with margarine. Cover and bake at 350 degrees for 35 to 40 minutes. Sprinkle marshmallows on top and broil until golden. Serves 6 to 8.

Make grown-ups feel like kids again! Stuff Christmas
stockings with penny candy, comic books,
card games like "Old Maid" and other childhood
delights...hang from the backs of dining room chairs
with tasseled cords.

Crockery Sage Dressing

Gina Rongved-Van Wyk
Rapid City, SD

How clever! Make stuffing in your slow cooker and free up the oven for other holiday dishes.

2 c. onion, chopped
2 c. celery, chopped
1 c. butter
2 loaves white bread, torn
1-1/2 t. dried sage
1 t. dried thyme

1/2 t. dried marjoram
1 t. poultry seasoning
1-1/2 t. salt
1/2 t. pepper
15-oz. can chicken broth
2 eggs, beaten

Sauté onion and celery in butter in a skillet; set aside. Place bread in a large mixing bowl; add seasonings and toss well. Add onion mixture and enough broth to moisten bread; toss well. Stir in eggs and mix well. Pour into a slow cooker. Cook, covered, on low setting for 4 to 8 hours, stirring occasionally and adding more broth as needed. Serves 10 to 12.

Decorate a grapevine wreath with tiny rag dolls and bears for a nostalgic look. Tie on a big bow of checked homespun...so cute!

Smokey Sausage & 2-Bean Soup

Rebecca Ross
Topeka, KS

I started out making minestrone and got carried away trying to create an extra-hearty soup for a cold winter day!

1/2 to 1 lb. smoked sausage,
   sliced
15-oz. can tomato sauce
2 15-oz. cans low-sodium
   beef broth
15-oz. can pinto beans,
   drained and rinsed
15-oz. can kidney beans,
   drained and rinsed
1/4 c. onion, chopped

1/4 c. celery, chopped
1/4 c. green pepper, chopped
1/4 c. red pepper, chopped
1 c. water
2 cubes beef bouillon
1/4 to 1/2 t. pepper
1/4 t. garlic salt
1/4 to 1/2 t. Italian seasoning
1 to 2 c. prepared rice

Combine all ingredients except rice in a slow cooker. Cover and cook on low setting for 2 to 8 hours. The longer this soup cooks, the richer the flavor will be. Stir in prepared rice 30 minutes before serving time; cover and cook an additional 30 minutes. Makes 8 to 10 servings.

Host a caroling party...gather up friends and serenade the neighbors! Back home, have slow cookers full of yummy soup and a hot beverage ready to warm everyone up. Add a platter of cookies for dessert and you're done!

Old-Fashioned Cornbread

Tonya Lightner
Bluffton, IN

No sour milk on hand? Buttermilk works equally well.

2 c. all-purpose flour
1 c. cornmeal
3 T. sugar
1 T. baking powder
3/4 t. baking soda

1 t. salt
2 eggs
3 T. oil
1-1/2 c. sour milk

Combine flour, cornmeal, sugar, baking powder, baking soda and salt; set aside. Mix eggs, oil and milk until smooth; stir into flour mixture. Spoon into a greased 9"x9" baking pan; bake at 350 degrees for 30 to 45 minutes. Serves 6 to 9.

Show your spirit with a star-spangled tree! Wind twinkly white lights and garlands of silver stars around the tree, then add shiny red and blue ornaments. Top with a cluster of mini American flags…how charming!

Quick Holiday Loaf

Margaret Strait
Whitehall, OH

Packed with delicious nuts and fruits!

1/2 c. currants
1/2 c. red and green candied
   cherries, chopped
1/2 c. dried pears, chopped
1/2 c. chopped walnuts
1 c. applesauce
1 c. sugar

2 eggs
1/2 c. oil
2 t. lemon zest
1-1/2 t. baking powder
1/2 t. baking soda
1/2 t. salt
2-1/4 c. all-purpose flour

Combine first 4 ingredients in a bowl; stir to mix. Reserve 1/2 cup for topping; set aside remaining mixture. Mix applesauce and sugar until sugar dissolves; beat in eggs, oil, lemon zest, baking powder, baking soda and salt until well blended. Stir in flour and fruit mixture; spread evenly into a greased 9"x5" loaf pan. Sprinkle with reserved fruit mixture. Bake at 325 degrees for one hour and 10 minutes, or until a knife tip comes out with moist crumbs attached. Cool in pan 10 minutes; run a knife around edges and invert onto a wire rack to cool completely. Makes one loaf.

Sing hey! Sing hey! for Christmas Day
Twine mistletoe and holly
For friendship glows in winter snows,
And so let's all be jolly.
-Old English Carol

Fireside
FAVORITES

Honey-Walnut Fruit Salad

Diane Cohen
Kennesaw, GA

Made of fruits that are available all winter, this salad is refreshing any time.

1/3 c. honey
1/2 c. light mayonnaise
3 apples, cored and chopped
2 bananas, sliced
1 c. seedless grapes

11-oz. can mandarin oranges, drained
1/2 c. chopped walnuts
1 c. lettuce, shredded
1 T. lemon juice

Blend honey and mayonnaise in a large bowl until smooth. Toss fruits, nuts and lettuce with lemon juice; add to honey mixture. Refrigerate. Makes 7 cups.

For a magical ice wreath, arrange cranberries and pine trimmings in a ring mold and fill with water. Freeze until solid, then pop out of the mold. Hang outdoors from a tree branch with a sturdy ribbon.

New Year's Day Soup

Becky Shoaf
Gatesville, TX

A bowl of this zesty soup will get you off to a good start!

1 carrot, peeled and chopped
1 stalk celery, chopped
1 c. cooked ham, cubed
2 T. olive oil
28-oz. can Italian plum
   tomatoes, chopped
4 c. water
2 cubes chicken bouillon
1/4 c. dried, minced onion
2 t. dried, minced garlic
1 t. dried oregano
1 t. dried basil

1/2 t. dried celery flakes
1/2 t. dried rosemary
1/8 t. red pepper flakes
1 bay leaf
3/4 t. salt
16-oz. pkg. frozen black-eyed
   peas
16-oz. pkg. frozen sliced okra
16-oz. pkg. frozen chopped
   turnips & turnip greens
1-1/4 c. small shell macaroni,
   uncooked

Sauté carrot, celery and ham with oil in a large stockpot over medium heat. Add tomatoes with juice, water, bouillon and seasonings; stir well. Add frozen vegetables; simmer over medium heat for 2 to 2-1/2 hours. Add macaroni; simmer an additional 10 minutes, until tender. Discard bay leaf. Makes 6 to 8 servings.

Swag a chandelier with ribbon-tied strings of beads to sparkle in candlelight. Check thrift stores for second-hand baubles or purchase carnival beads at a local party supply store.

Fireside FAVORITES

Black-Eyed Pea Cornbread

Susan Moseley
Pine Bluff, AR

Hearty and filling...almost a meal in itself!

1 lb. ground pork sausage
1 onion, chopped
1 c. cornmeal
1 t. salt
1/2 t. baking soda
2/3 c. all-purpose flour
1 c. buttermilk

2 eggs, beaten
1/2 c. oil
1/4 c. cream-style corn
8-oz. pkg. shredded Cheddar
  cheese
15-oz. can black-eyed peas,
  drained and rinsed

Brown sausage and onion; drain and set aside. Combine cornmeal, salt, baking soda and flour in a bowl; add buttermilk, eggs and oil. Stir in sausage mixture and remaining ingredients; mix well. Pour into a greased 13"x9" baking pan. Bake at 350 degrees for 50 to 55 minutes, or until golden. Serves 8 to 12.

Hot glue small pine cones, nuts or seed pods to a styrofoam cone for a quick & easy tabletop tree. Spray with gold paint or leave it natural.

Snow Grapes

Charla Coble
Glenford, OH

Mix red and white grapes for a pretty contrast.

8-oz. pkg. cream cheese,
   softened
8-oz. container sour cream

3/4 c. sugar
1 t. vanilla extract
1 to 2 lbs. seedless grapes

Mix together all ingredients except grapes. Fold in grapes; chill for at least 4 hours. Serves 4 to 6.

Christmas Cranberry Salad

Jennifer Batcheller
Bishop, CA

Tart and crunchy!

12-oz. pkg. cranberries
2 oranges, peeled, seeded
   and chopped

zest of one orange
1 c. sugar
1/4 c. chopped pecans

Place cranberries in a food processor or blender and process until berries are finely chopped. Add remaining ingredients; chill for 24 hours. Serves 6 to 8.

Mix & match clear glass hurricanes for an oh-so-easy centerpiece. Fitted with candles all in the same color, they'll make a cheerful burst of candlelight.

Favorite Pineapple-Lime Salad

Kay Marone
Des Moines, IA

A tradition at our Christmas dinner table.

14 marshmallows
1 c. milk
6-oz. pkg. lime gelatin mix
8-oz. pkg. cream cheese,
   softened

10.8-oz. pkg. whipped topping
   mix
20-oz. can crushed pineapple
14-1/2 oz. jar maraschino
   cherries, drained

Combine marshmallows and milk in a saucepan. Cook over low heat until marshmallows melt; cool. Transfer marshmallow mixture to a large bowl. Add remaining ingredients except cherries and mix well with an electric mixer on low speed. Stir in cherries. Cover and chill. Serves 8 to 10.

Make ribbon candy ornaments that look just like the real thing! Take 18 inches of wide striped grosgrain ribbon and fold accordion-style, then insert a threaded needle through the center. Knot both ends and make a loop for hanging. Sweet!

Slow-Cooker Beef Stew

Lori Czarnecki
Milwaukee, WI

A family favorite...we have plenty of chilly days here in Wisconsin!

1 lb. redskin potatoes, quartered
1-1/2 c. frozen pearl onions
16-oz. pkg. baby carrots
1-1/2 lbs. beef stew meat, cubed

3 T. all-purpose flour
12-oz. jar beef gravy
14-1/2 oz. can diced tomatoes

Layer potatoes, onions and carrots in a slow cooker. Add beef; sprinkle with flour. Top with gravy and tomatoes. Cover and cook on low setting for 8 to 10 hours. Serves 4 to 6.

Chicken Corn Chowder

Brenda Kauffman
Harrisburg, PA

A dear friend gave me this recipe...she added zing to ordinary corn chowder with Mexican-blend cheese.

3 c. cooked chicken, diced
2 c. carrots, peeled, sliced
   and cooked
2 12-oz. cans sweet corn &
   green peppers
2 10-3/4 oz. cans cream of
   potato soup

4 c. milk
2 cubes chicken bouillon
1/2 t. celery seed
salt and pepper to taste
8-oz. pkg. shredded Mexican-
   blend cheese

Combine all ingredients except cheese in a slow cooker. Cover and cook on low setting for 4 to 5 hours. Stir in cheese just before serving. Makes 8 to 10 servings.

A simmering kettle of soup fills the house with a wonderful aroma...so relaxing when you're wrapping gifts or writing Christmas cards!

Homemade Macaroni & Cheese

Brenda Douglass
North Cape May, NJ

Just like Mom used to make...real comfort food!

1/4 c. margarine, melted
1/4 c. all-purpose flour
2 c. milk
8-oz. pkg. extra-sharp white
　　Cheddar cheese, diced

salt and pepper to taste
8-oz. pkg. elbow macaroni,
　　cooked

Melt margarine in a saucepan; remove from heat. Add flour and stir until smooth; gradually stir in milk. Over medium heat, cook and stir constantly until thickened. Add cheese; reduce heat and cook, stirring occasionally until smooth. Stir in salt and pepper to taste. Combine cheese mixture with cooked macaroni and place in a greased 13"x9" baking pan. Bake at 350 degrees until golden, 45 to 50 minutes. Serves 8 to 10.

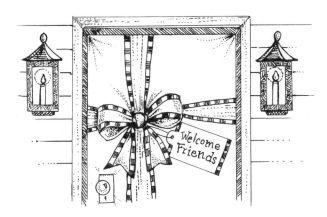

Wrap your front door like a giant gift box! It's easy with a plastic party tablecloth and clear tape. Add a big ribbon bow and an oversized gift tag that says "Welcome Friends!"

Savory Spinach

Jennifer Eveland-Kupp
Temple, PA

Creamy baked spinach...scrumptious!

3 10-oz. pkgs. frozen chopped   8-oz. container sour cream
  spinach, cooked and drained   1-1/2 oz. pkg. onion soup mix

Mix together all ingredients; place in a greased 2-quart casserole dish.
Bake at 350 degrees for 30 minutes. Serves 8 to 10.

Creamy Dijon Mushrooms

Dorothy Armijo
Dallas, TX

Friends always ask, "Are you bringing those mushrooms?"

1/3 c. butter, softened   1/8 t. nutmeg
1-1/2 T. all-purpose flour   1/8 t. cayenne pepper
1 T. Dijon mustard   16-oz. pkg. mushrooms,
1 T. fresh parsley, minced   stems removed
1 t. salt   1 c. whipping cream
1 T. onion, minced

Blend butter, flour, mustard and seasonings together; set aside.
Place mushrooms in a greased one-quart casserole dish; dot with
butter mixture. Pour cream over the top; bake at 375 degrees for
one hour. Serves 4.

Toss a red & white
patterned quilt over the
sofa for instant
Christmas warmth.

Parmesan Pull-Aparts

Diane Cohen
Kennesaw, GA

Three kinds of savory seeds really dress up ordinary biscuits.

3 T. margarine
1 T. onion, minced
2 t. dill seed
1 t. poppy seed

1/4 t. celery seed
10-oz. tube refrigerated biscuits,
   quartered
1/4 t. grated Parmesan cheese

Melt margarine in a 9" round cake pan. Sprinkle onion, dill, poppy and celery seed over margarine. Sprinkle quartered biscuits with Parmesan and arrange in pan. Bake at 400 degrees for 15 to 18 minutes. To serve, invert pan over a serving platter and turn out biscuits.
Makes 10.

Include every member of the family (regardless of age)
in a photo with Santa...the resulting picture
will be priceless!

Spinach Bread

Julie Fitzgerald
Anacoco, LA

My step-mom, Carol, shared this yummy recipe with me.

6-oz. pkg. baby spinach,
   chopped
1/4 c. butter
1 c. all-purpose flour
1/2 t. baking powder

salt and pepper to taste
2 eggs, beaten
1/2 c. milk
8-oz. pkg. shredded Monterey
   Jack cheese

Rinse and drain spinach; place in a microwave-safe bowl. Microwave on high setting for one to 2 minutes; set aside. Melt butter in a 9"x9" baking pan. Arrange spinach over butter, pressing down. Sift together flour, baking powder, salt and pepper. Add eggs and milk; whisk until mixture is smooth. Sprinkle cheese over spinach and top with flour mixture. Bake at 375 degrees for 40 minutes, or until top is bubbly and golden. Cut into squares. Serves 6 to 9.

Evergreen wreaths aren't for doors only! Use a big red velvet ribbon to suspend a wreath in front of a window...try hanging 3 wreaths in front of a picture window.

Chicken Rice Pilaf

Jan Swartzel
Canal Fulton, OH

A tasty side dish for chicken or pork.

1/2 c. margarine
1/2 c. angel hair pasta, broken
    into 1-inch pieces, uncooked
14-1/2 oz. can chicken broth
1 c. water

1 c. long-cooking rice, uncooked
1 cube chicken bouillon
1 t. salt
Optional: 4-oz. can sliced
    mushrooms, drained

Melt margarine in a skillet over medium heat. Add uncooked pasta; cook and stir until golden. Stir in broth, water, rice, bouillon and salt. Add mushrooms, if using. Cover and cook over low heat for 30 minutes to one hour, until liquid has been absorbed. Serves 4.

Reproductions of nostalgic holiday postcards make charming gift tags! Simply punch a hole in one end and tie onto a package. The reverse side of the card offers plenty of space for the recipient's name and a holiday message.

Date-Nut Bread in a Coffee Can

Nancy Wise
Little Rock, AR

A favorite for gift-giving...oh-so-easy in a slow cooker!

3/4 c. dates, finely chopped
1/2 to 1 c. chopped pecans
1 c. all-purpose flour, divided
1/4 c. brown sugar, packed
2 t. baking powder
1/4 t. baking soda
1/2 t. salt

1/2 t. mace or nutmeg
3/4 c. milk
1 egg, beaten
1 T. oil
1 T. orange zest
1/2 c. whole-wheat flour
3 c. hot water

Toss dates and pecans with 1/4 cup flour; set aside. In a large bowl, mix remaining flour, brown sugar, baking powder, baking soda, salt and mace or nutmeg; set aside. In a separate bowl, whisk together milk, egg, oil and orange zest. Add to flour mixture alternating with whole-wheat flour; mix well. Fold in date mixture. Pour into a greased and floured one-pound coffee can; cover tightly with aluminum foil. Set can on a rack or trivet in a slow cooker; pour hot water around can. Cover and cook on high setting for 2-1/2 to 3-1/2 hours. Do not lift lid before 2 hours. Makes one loaf.

Trim a doll-size
Christmas tree with
mini ornaments...it's
just the right size for
a holiday buffet
table. Sweet!

Fireside
FAVORITES

Winter Salad with Dijon Dressing

Jana Warnell
Kalispell, MT

An irresistible mix of flavors.

1 to 2 heads romaine, red leaf,
   and/or green leaf lettuce
1 apple, cored and chopped
1 red onion, chopped

1/2 c. sweetened, dried
   cranberries
1/2 c. sliced almonds
1/2 c. crumbled blue cheese

Toss together lettuce, apple and onion with Dijon Dressing in a large salad bowl. Sprinkle with remaining ingredients. Amounts can be adjusted according to your taste and how much you want to make. Serves 6 to 8.

Dijon Dressing:

3/4 c. olive oil
3 T. sherry wine vinegar

3 T. lemon juice
1 T. Dijon mustard

Whisk together all ingredients.

Gifts of time and love are surely the basic
ingredients of a truly merry Christmas.
-Peg Bracken

Mama's Garlic Bread

Marla Arbet
Burlington, WI

Absolutely delicious...my husband says it's ooey-gooey!

2 cloves garlic, minced
1/4 c. grated Parmesan cheese
1/4 c. Romano cheese, shredded
1/4 c. butter, softened
1/4 c. olive oil

1/4 c. mayonnaise
2 T. fresh parsley, chopped
1/4 t. dried oregano
1 to 2 loaves Italian bread,
   halved lengthwise

Mix garlic, cheeses, butter, oil, mayonnaise, parsley and oregano; spread over bread. Wrap in aluminum foil; bake at 375 degrees for 15 minutes. Unwrap; broil for 2 to 3 minutes. Serves 6 to 8.

Parmesan Cheese Loaf

Pam Astin
Powder Springs, GA

Wonderful with pasta dishes.

1/2 c. margarine, softened
1/2 c. grated Parmesan cheese

1 loaf French bread, halved
   lengthwise

Mix margarine and cheese together. Spread on French bread and bake on an ungreased baking sheet at 350 degrees, until golden. Slice to serve. Makes about one dozen slices.

Tuck in the kids with visions of sugarplums...stitch up some simple pillowcases from holiday fabric.

Rumbledethumps

*Jane Finn
Gurnee, IL*

A funny Scottish name for a hearty, satisfying dish! Add some crispy bacon to turn it into a main dish.

1 lb. potatoes, peeled and diced
2 T. butter
1 onion, thinly sliced
1/2 lb. cabbage, finely shredded

salt and pepper to taste
2/3 c. shredded Cheddar cheese, divided

Cover potatoes with water in a saucepan; bring to a boil. Reduce heat; cover and simmer for 8 minutes, or until just tender. Drain and rinse under cold water; drain again. Transfer potatoes to a bowl; mash coarsely with a fork and set aside. Heat butter in a skillet; add onion and cook over low heat for 10 minutes, or until soft. Add cabbage; cook for 5 minutes. Stir in potatoes, salt and pepper. Remove from heat; stir in 2 tablespoons cheese. Transfer to a greased 9"x9" baking pan; sprinkle with remaining cheese. Bake at 350 degrees for 20 minutes. Serves 4 to 6.

Take a walk around the garden with a basket and a pair of snips. You may find evergreen branches, sprigs of berries or even bare twigs that can be tucked into a winter arrangement.

Dutch Farmers' Cheese Soup

Lisa Chrisco
Arnold, MO

An old-fashioned soup that's perfect for winter.

1/4 c. butter
1-1/2 lbs. potatoes, peeled
   and diced
1-1/2 lbs. cauliflower flowerets
1 lb. carrots, peeled and sliced

1 onion, chopped
4 to 5 c. vegetable broth
salt and pepper
6 thick slices French bread
3/4 lb. Gouda cheese, sliced

Melt butter in a Dutch oven over medium-high heat. Add vegetables and sauté until onion is golden, about 7 minutes. Add broth; bring to a boil. Reduce heat; simmer for 30 minutes, or until veggies are tender, adding more broth if soup is too thick. Season to taste with salt and pepper. Transfer soup to one large or 6 individual oven-safe bowls. Arrange bread slices on top of soup. Place cheese slices over bread, covering completely. Broil 6 inches from heat source until cheese is melted and golden. Serves 6.

Hang a pair of ice skates and a pair of woolly mittens
on the front door with a big bow!

Christmas Pistachio Bread

Michelle Campen
Peoria, IL

Sweet and tender, yet oh-so-simple to make!

18-1/2 oz. pkg. yellow cake mix
3.4-oz. pkg. instant pistachio
    pudding mix
4 eggs, beaten
1/2 c. oil

1/4 c. water
8-oz. container sour cream
1/4 c. sugar
1 t. cinnamon

Combine first 6 ingredients in a large bowl; mix well. Pour into two, greased 9"x5" loaf pans; set aside. Mix sugar and cinnamon together and sprinkle evenly over top, pressing into batter. Bake at 350 degrees for 40 minutes. Makes 2 loaves.

Turn mini terra cotta flowerpots into holiday bell ornaments in a snap. Paint in Christmasy colors, then tie a jingle bell onto a ribbon and insert through the hole in the bottom of the pot.

Chunky Potato Soup

Dawn Van Horn
Columbia, NC

Pack a thermos of this hearty soup and go on a winter snow hike.

2 c. water
3 redskin potatoes, peeled
   and cut into 1-inch cubes
3 T. butter
1 onion, finely chopped
3 T. all-purpose flour

salt and red pepper flakes
   to taste
3 c. milk
1/2 t. sugar
1 c. shredded Cheddar cheese
1 c. cooked ham, cubed

Bring water to a boil in a medium Dutch oven; add potatoes and cook until tender. Drain; reserving one cup liquid; set potatoes aside. Melt butter in a skillet over medium heat; add onion and sauté until tender. Add flour, salt and red pepper flakes to taste; cook and stir over low heat for 3 to 4 minutes. Add potatoes, reserved cooking liquid, milk and sugar; stir well and simmer until hot. Add cheese and ham; simmer over low heat until cheese is melted. Makes 6 to 8 servings.

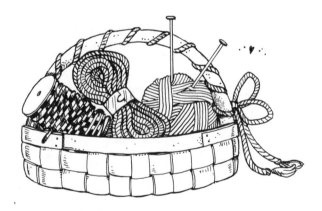

No more ordinary ribbon! Visit a knitting shop for yarns in exciting colors and textures that will make gifts stand out under the tree. Bulky yarns are perfect...thin yarns can be doubled or tripled.

Golden Parmesan Roasted Potatoes

Linda Hendrix
Moundville, MO

Pop into the oven alongside a roast.

1/4 c. all-purpose flour
1/4 c. grated Parmesan cheese
3/4 t. salt
1/8 t. pepper

6 potatoes, peeled and
   cut into wedges
1/3 c. butter, melted
Garnish: fresh parsley, chopped

Place flour, cheese, salt and pepper in a plastic zipping bag; mix well. Add potato wedges; shake to coat. Pour butter into a 13"x9" baking pan; arrange potatoes in pan. Bake at 375 degrees for one hour. Sprinkle with parsley. Serves 4 to 6.

Angel Cream Biscuits

Teresa Parton
Alexandria, VA

They melt in your mouth!

1 env. active dry yeast
1/4 c. warm water
1 T. sugar

2 c. biscuit baking mix
1/4 c. half-and-half

In a medium bowl, dissolve yeast in warm water, about 110 to 115 degrees. Stir in sugar, then remaining ingredients; stir until dough forms. Turn onto surface generously dusted with biscuit baking mix; gently roll to coat. Shape into ball and knead 10 times; roll 1/2-inch thick. Cut with a biscuit cutter dipped in biscuit baking mix; place on ungreased baking sheet. Cover and let stand in a warm place for about 30 minutes, until soft and puffy. Bake at 425 degrees for 6 to 8 minutes, until golden. Serve warm. Makes 10 to 12.

Heap a vintage copper washtub
with logs by the hearth...the
copper will gleam in the firelight.

Holiday Sweet Potato Puffs

Shellie Pool
Haysville, KS

Favorite flavors, served in a fun new way!

4 c. sweet potatoes, peeled,
   cooked and mashed
2/3 c. brown sugar, packed

1 t. orange zest
8 marshmallows
2 c. sweetened flaked coconut

Combine sweet potatoes, brown sugar and zest. Shape 1/2 cup of mixture around each marshmallow, forming a ball. Roll each ball in coconut; place in a greased 13"x9" baking pan. Bake at 350 degrees for 15 minutes. Makes 8 servings.

Take the family to a local tree farm and cut your own Christmas tree! Afterwards, warm up with mugs of hot cocoa. You'll be creating sweet memories!

Sweets to SHARE

Granny's Christmas Cake

Sharen Simmons
Lincoln, NE

My granny was a wonderful cook! All of us grandkids have special memories of her great sense of humor and her delicious desserts.

2 c. all-purpose flour
1-1/2 c. sugar
2 T. baking cocoa
1-1/2 t. baking soda
1-1/2 t. salt
1/2 t. ground cloves
1/2 t. cinnamon
1/2 t. nutmeg

1/2 t. allspice
1/2 c. shortening
1-1/2 c. applesauce
2 eggs, beaten
1/2 c. raisins
1/2 c. chopped dates
3/4 c. chopped walnuts

In a large bowl, combine all ingredients except raisins, dates and walnuts; mix well. Add raisins, dates and walnuts; stir just until combined. Spread in a greased 8" tube pan and bake at 350 degrees for about 1-1/2 hours, or in a greased 13"x9" baking pan for 55 to 65 minutes. Cool completely; frost with Cranberry Frosting. Serves 12.

Cranberry Frosting:

2 T. shortening
1 T. margarine, softened
1 t. vanilla extract
1/4 t. salt

3 T. cranberry juice cocktail
1 T. milk
3 c. powdered sugar
Optional: red food coloring

Mix together all ingredients except powdered sugar. Add powdered sugar and mix well. Add red food coloring, if desired.

A joy that's shared is a joy
made double.
-English Proverb

Sweets to SHARE

Marshmallow Roll

Sandra Robbins
Topeka, KS

A real old-fashioned treat.

1/2 c. sweetened
   condensed milk
1/4 c. water
32 marshmallows, quartered
1/2 c. chopped walnuts

1/2 c. chopped dates
2-1/2 c. graham cracker crumbs
Garnish: frozen whipped
   topping, thawed

Mix condensed milk and water in a medium bowl; stir in remaining ingredients except whipped topping. Shape into a 6-inch by 3-inch roll; wrap in plastic wrap and refrigerate for at least 12 hours. Slice to desired thickness; top slices with a dollop of whipped topping. Serves 6 to 8.

Take the kids to a local ceramic painting shop. They'll love designing and decorating a plate and mug especially for Santa's milk and cookies!

Snowball Cookies

Sandi Grock
Huntsville, TX

You may know these tender cookies as Russian Teacakes.

1 c. butter, softened
1/2 c. powdered sugar
1 t. vanilla extract
2-1/2 c. all-purpose flour

1/4 t. salt
3/4 c. chopped pecans
Garnish: powdered sugar

Combine butter and sugar in a large bowl; blend until light and fluffy. Stir in vanilla; set aside. Sift together flour and salt; add to butter mixture and mix well. Stir in nuts. Shape into one-inch balls; place on ungreased baking sheets. Bake at 350 degrees for 15 minutes. Roll cookies in powdered sugar while still hot. Let cool and roll again in powdered sugar. Makes about 3 dozen.

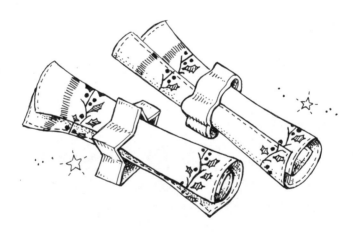

Cookie cutters make clever napkin rings…just slip the rolled-up napkin through the center. With a different shape for each person, it's oh-so easy to know whose napkin is whose.

Merry Reindeer Cookies

Debi Piper
Vicksburg, MI

The kids will love decorating these cookies!

17-1/2 oz. pkg. peanut butter
   cookie mix
1/3 c. oil
1 egg, beaten

60 mini pretzel twists
60 semi-sweet chocolate chips
30 red cinnamon candies

Combine cookie mix, oil and egg in a mixing bowl. Beat until well mixed. Shape into a 7-1/2 inch roll; wrap in plastic wrap. Chill for one hour; unwrap and cut into 1/4-inch slices. Place cookies about 2 inches apart on ungreased baking sheets. Using thumb and forefinger, make a slight indentation one-third of the way down the sides of each slice. Press in pretzels for antlers, chocolate chips for eyes and red hots for noses. Bake at 350 degrees for 9 to 11 minutes, or until golden. Remove to wire racks to cool. Makes 2-1/2 dozen.

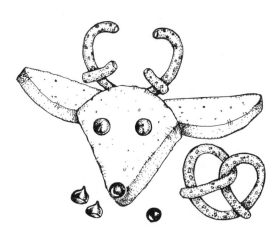

For the quickest-ever candy treats, top waffle-shaped pretzels with a dollop of white frosting…sprinkle with mini red candy-coated chocolates. Yummy!

Shannon's Faux Pralines

Stephen Ratterman
Louisville, KY

Really delicious and oh-so easy to make.

1 sleeve graham crackers	1/2 c. sugar
1/2 c. butter	1/8 t. salt
1/2 c. margarine	1 c. chopped pecans

Cover a baking sheet with aluminum foil; spray lightly with non-stick vegetable spray. Break crackers coarsely and arrange on baking sheet. Set aside. Melt butter, margarine, sugar and salt together in a saucepan over low heat. Bring to a boil and boil for 2 minutes; pour over crackers. Sprinkle pecans over top; bake at 350 degrees for 10 to 12 minutes. Let cool; break apart. Makes 4 to 6 servings.

Show off 3 or 4 of Grandmother's most treasured Christmas ornaments…hang them on a countertop coffee mug holder. Finish with a few twists of tinsel.

Cherry Snowballs

Karrie Middaugh
Salt Lake City, UT

Surprise! There's a maraschino cherry tucked inside.

1 c. butter, softened
2-1/2 c. powdered sugar, divided
1 T. water
1 t. vanilla extract
2 c. all-purpose flour
1 c. quick-cooking oats,
   uncooked

1/2 t. salt
36 maraschino cherries, drained
1/4 to 1/3 c. milk
2 c. sweetened flaked coconut,
   finely chopped

Blend butter, 1/2 cup powdered sugar, water and vanilla in a large bowl; set aside. Combine flour, oats and salt; gradually add to butter mixture. Shape a tablespoonful of dough around each cherry, forming a ball. Arrange balls 2 inches apart on ungreased baking sheets. Bake at 350 degrees for 18 to 20 minutes, until golden on bottoms. Remove to a wire rack to cool. Combine remaining powdered sugar and enough milk to make a smooth dipping consistency. Dip cookies; roll in coconut. Makes 3 dozen.

Homemade candy is always a welcome gift! Make the
gift even sweeter…place individual candies in mini
paper muffin cups and arrange in a decorated box.

Chocolate Spritz

Sara Tatham
Plymouth, NH

One busy year, our 3rd-grade daughter, Carrie, saved our Christmas cookie tradition by mixing up all the different batches of dough herself. These are some of the cookies that she made.

3/4 c. butter, softened
1 c. sugar
1 egg, beaten
2 T. milk
1/2 t. vanilla extract

2 c. all-purpose flour
6 T. baking cocoa
1/4 t. salt
Garnish: candy sprinkles

Beat butter in a large bowl until creamy. Gradually add sugar; beat until fluffy. Mix in egg, milk and vanilla until well blended. Sift together remaining ingredients except candy sprinkles. Slowly stir flour mixture into butter mixture. Shape dough into one-inch balls; roll in sprinkles. Arrange on an ungreased baking sheet and bake at 375 degrees for 8 to 10 minutes. Makes about 4 dozen.

Snowy paper-white narcissus flowers are a winter delight that Grandmother loved. Place paper-white bulbs pointed-side up in water-filled bulb vases. Place in a sunny window. In about 6 weeks you'll have blooms!

Goody Gumdrop Cookies

Kristine Marumoto
Sandy, UT

Here's a little trick to make evenly sized balls of dough...just use a small ice cream scoop.

3/4 c. shortening
1 c. brown sugar, packed
1 c. sugar
2 eggs, beaten
1 T. vanilla extract
2 c. all-purpose flour
1 T. baking soda

1 T. baking powder
1/4 t. salt
2 c. quick-cooking oats, uncooked
1 c. mini gumdrops
1 c. sweetened flaked coconut

Blend shortening and sugars together in a large mixing bowl. Add eggs and vanilla; mix well and set aside. Sift together flour, baking soda, baking powder and salt; mix in oats. Stir flour mixture into shortening mixture to make a thick batter. Fold in gumdrops and coconut. Drop by tablespoonfuls onto lightly greased baking sheets. Bake at 375 degrees for 10 minutes. Makes 3 dozen.

Wrap a stack of cookies in tinted plastic wrap and place in a holiday mug. Tuck in several packets of flavored creamer and voilà, a gift that co-workers will appreciate!

Date Loaf

Flo Burtnett
Gage, OK

My mother always used to make this dessert at Christmas time...it's one of my most delicious memories.

16-oz. pkg. chopped dates
16-oz. pkg. mini marshmallows
1 c. chopped nuts

16-oz. pkg. graham crackers, finely crushed and divided
1 pt. light cream

Mix dates, marshmallows and nuts in a large bowl. Stir in cream and graham cracker crumbs, reserving one cup crumbs. Mix well and shape into a 12-inch loaf or roll. Sprinkle reserved crumbs on a sheet of wax paper; roll loaf in crumbs. Refrigerate for several hours; slice into 1/2-inch thick pieces and serve. Makes about 2 dozen.

Make a living rosemary wreath for your favorite cook!
Insert a circle of wire in a potted rosemary plant and
use thread to train stems onto the wire. In just a few
weeks, new growth will fill out the shape of the wreath.

Sweets to SHARE

White Texas Sheet Cake

*Carole Snodgrass
Rolla, MO*

A moist, yummy cake that's big enough for a crowd!

1 c. butter
1 c. water
2 c. all-purpose flour
2 c. sugar
2 eggs, beaten

1/2 c. sour cream
1 t. almond extract
1 t. salt
1 t. baking soda

Bring butter and water to a boil in a large saucepan. Remove from heat. Add remaining ingredients; stir until smooth. Pour into a greased 15"x10" jelly-roll pan. Bake at 350 degrees for 20 to 22 minutes, or until cake is golden and tests done. Cool for 20 minutes; spread frosting over warm cake. Makes 24 servings.

Frosting:

1/2 c. butter
1/4 c. milk
4-1/2 c. powdered sugar

1/2 t. almond extract
1 c. chopped walnuts

Combine butter and milk in a saucepan; bring to a boil. Remove from heat; add sugar and almond extract. Mix well and stir in walnuts.

Have fun with mini cookie cutters! Decorate a cake with fruit leather cut-outs, make vents in a pot pie crust or garnish an appetizer tray with Cheddar cheese stars.

Cran-Apple Cobbler

Kimberly Blackwell
Pensacola, FL

Top with scoops of vanilla ice cream for an extra treat!

4 Granny Smith apples, peeled,
   cored and thinly sliced
16-oz. can whole-berry
   cranberry sauce

18-oz. tube refrigerated sugar
   cookie dough, sliced
1/4-inch thick

Combine apples and cranberry sauce in a mixing bowl; mix well.
Place in a greased 8"x8" baking pan; arrange slices of cookie dough
on top. Bake at 350 degrees for 20 minutes, or until bubbly and
golden. Serves 6.

When you wrap up cookies for family & friends,
remember to make one more plate, tag it "Welcome,
Neighbor!" and hand-deliver it to somebody who's
new in town.

Creamy Rice Pudding

Susie O'Sell
Albert Lea, MN

A Christmas Eve tradition in my family...an almond is hidden in the pudding and the lucky person who finds it gets a prize!

4 c. milk
1/2 c. long-cooking rice,
   uncooked
1/2 c. whipping cream

1/2 c. sugar
1 t. vanilla extract
Optional: cinnamon

Combine milk and rice in a lightly greased 2-quart casserole dish. Bake at 350 degrees for 2 hours without stirring. Just before serving, add cream, sugar and vanilla. Sprinkle with cinnamon, if desired. Serve warm. Makes 4 servings.

Bake up a batch of gingerbread boys and girls, then let the kids decorate them! Set out a variety of small candies along with tubs of frosting. You'll be amazed by how creative kids can be!

Christmas-Time Orange Balls

Jennifer Halsmer
Franklin, IN

My Granny Jo and I always used to spend a wonderful day making homemade candies and confections at Christmas.

12-oz. pkg. vanilla wafers, finely crushed
16-oz. pkg. powdered sugar
6-oz. can frozen orange juice concentrate, thawed
1/2 c. butter, softened
1 c. pecans, finely chopped
Garnish: additional chopped pecans or sweetened flaked coconut

Combine all ingredients except garnish, mixing well. Shape into one-inch balls; roll in chopped pecans or coconut. Makes 5 to 6 dozen.

Chocolate-Covered Cherries

Diane Madej
Amsterdam, NY

A candy-box favorite!

3 10-oz. jars maraschino cherries with stems, drained
3 T. margarine, softened
3 T. light corn syrup
2 c. powdered sugar
1 lb. melting chocolate

Drain cherries on paper towels for several hours. Combine margarine and corn syrup in a medium bowl; stir in powdered sugar. Shape 1/2 teaspoon mixture around each cherry; chill for one hour, or until firm. Melt chocolate in a double boiler over low heat; dip cherries into chocolate and chill. Store in an airtight container; allow candy to ripen one to 2 weeks so that liquid centers can develop. Makes 5 dozen.

Turn mini pretzels into delicious candy box treats...simply dip in melted chocolate!

Santa's Peanut Butter Fudge

Sandy Ward
Anderson, IN

Grandma made these extra special with a pecan half on each square.

2/3 c. milk
2 c. sugar
1 c. mini marshmallows

1 c. crunchy peanut butter
1 t. vanilla extract
1/2 c. chopped dates

Combine milk and sugar in a saucepan over medium-high heat. Bring to a boil without stirring until a candy thermometer registers 240 degrees, or a soft ball forms in cold water. Remove from heat; add marshmallows, peanut butter, vanilla and dates. Stir just until combined. Pour into a lightly greased 8"x8" pan; refrigerate at least 20 minutes before cutting. Makes 12 to 15 pieces.

Add a handwritten recipe card when giving a tin of family favorites like fudge or cookies...the gift will be appreciated twice as much!

Peppermint Snowballs

Mike Watts
Dayton, OH

So simple...so yummy!

18-oz. pkg. chocolate sandwich
   cookies, finely crushed
8-oz. pkg. cream cheese,
   softened

6-oz. pkg. white melting
   chocolate
1 to 1-1/2 c. peppermint
   candies, finely crushed

Mix together crushed cookies and cream cheese. Roll into 1-1/2 inch
balls and set aside. Melt white chocolate in the top of a double boiler
over low heat; stir in crushed candy. Dip balls into chocolate and set
on wax paper to harden. Makes 2-1/2 dozen.

Patchwork Christmas stockings are a sweet way to share
an old quilt that's become very worn. Cut simple
stocking shapes from the best portions of the quilt,
stitch together and trim with tea-dyed lace.

Merry Christmas Bars

Linda Walker
Erie, CO

*Wrap several bars in tinted plastic wrap and
tie with a ribbon for a delightful lunchbox surprise.*

3/4 c. raisins
3/4 c. semi-sweet
　chocolate chips
1/2 c. chopped walnuts
1/2 c. maraschino cherry
　halves, drained
1 c. plus 2 T. all-purpose
　flour, divided

1/3 c. butter, softened
1-1/2 c. brown sugar, packed
2 eggs
1 t. vanilla extract
1 t. baking powder
1 t. salt

Combine raisins, chocolate chips, nuts and cherries with 2 tablespoons flour; set aside. Blend butter, brown sugar and eggs until fluffy. Add vanilla; mix well. Sift together remaining flour, baking powder and salt; add to butter mixture, blending well. Stir in raisin mixture. Spread in a lightly greased 11"x7" baking pan. Bake at 350 degrees for about 40 minutes, or until a toothpick comes out clean when inserted in the center. Cool in pan; cut into bars. Makes about 2 dozen.

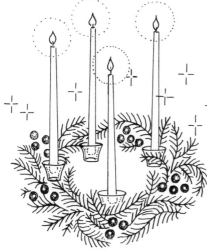

Make an Advent wreath to count the weeks to Christmas. Lay an evergreen wreath flat and space 4 taper candles around it. Each Sunday before Christmas, light an additional candle.

Christmas Cut-Out Cookies

Mary Emmons
Lyman, ME

My family always gets together to make cookies and homemade ice cream at Christmas...what memories!

3 c. all-purpose flour	1 c. shortening
1 t. baking powder	2 eggs
1 t. baking soda	1/4 c. milk
1 t. salt	2 t. vanilla extract
1-1/2 c. sugar	

In a large bowl, sift together first 5 ingredients; set aside. Mix together remaining ingredients in another large bowl. Gradually add flour mixture to shortening mixture to form a very soft dough. On a well-floured board, knead in some flour; roll out to desired thickness and cut out with cookie cutters. Place on lightly greased baking sheets; bake at 375 degrees for 6 to 7 minutes. Makes 4 to 5 dozen.

Sugar Cookie Frosting

Brenda Smith
Gooseberry Patch

Mix up several bowls in different colors!

1 c. powdered sugar	several drops food coloring
3-1/2 t. milk	2 t. light corn syrup
1/4 t. vanilla extract	

Stir together powdered sugar, milk, vanilla and food coloring in a small bowl. Add corn syrup; stir until smooth and glossy. If too thick, add a little more corn syrup. Use frosting immediately; let cookies dry completely before stacking. Makes about one cup.

Let the kids get creative with cookie frosting! Set out a small new paintbrush for each color.

Minty Meringues

Carlita Zummo
Port Arthur, TX

Add a drop or 2 of red food coloring for pretty pink meringues.

2 egg whites
1/2 t. vanilla extract
1/8 t. cream of tartar

2/3 c. sugar
1/4 c. peppermint candies,
    finely crushed

In a medium bowl, let egg whites stand at room temperature for one hour. Add vanilla and cream of tartar; beat with an electric mixer on medium speed until soft peaks form. Add sugar one tablespoon at a time; beat on high speed until sugar dissolves and stiff peaks form. Gently fold in crushed candies. Drop by rounded teaspoonfuls 1-1/2 inches apart on greased baking sheets. Bake at 325 degrees for 10 to 12 minutes, until set. Turn off oven; let meringues dry in oven with door closed for 20 minutes. Remove from baking sheets; store in an airtight container. Makes 2-1/2 dozen.

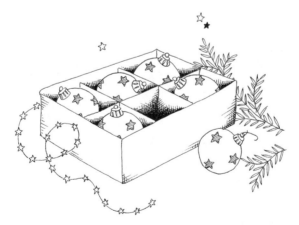

Spruce up glass ornaments that have lost their shine!
Simply brush with craft glue and sprinkle with fine
glitter. Add hanging loops of colorful ribbon or
metallic cord...better than new!

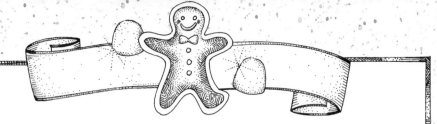

Cranberry Mousse Parfaits

Kim Koyle
Victorville, CA

Our family has enjoyed this recipe for 20 years.

2 6-oz. pkgs. raspberry
    gelatin mix
32-oz. bottle cranberry juice
    cocktail

16-oz. can whole-berry
    cranberry sauce
12-oz. container frozen
    whipped topping, thawed

Prepare gelatin following package directions, but using cranberry juice instead of water. Divide gelatin mixture between 2 bowls; stir cranberry sauce into first bowl. Place both bowls in refrigerator until thickened. Remove from refrigerator; set aside cranberry sauce mixture. Fold whipped topping into second bowl. Layer in 8 dessert glasses, alternating cranberry sauce mixture with whipped topping mixture until glasses are full. Refrigerate until ready to serve. Makes 8 parfaits.

Save the round metal ends from refrigerated biscuit tubes to make mini punched tin ornaments. Simply lay them on a wooden board and pierce with a hammer and nail to form a simple star or snowflake design. Insert a ribbon for hanging.

Sweets to SHARE

Mom's Christmas Cake

Stephanie Stiebel
Festus, MO

My mom makes this cake every Christmas…it's perfect for the holidays with the red and green colors swirling through it. My brother's birthday is on Christmas, so this is his birthday cake too!

18-1/2 oz. pkg. white cake mix
3-oz. pkg. cherry gelatin mix
3-oz. pkg. lime gelatin mix
2 c. boiling water, divided

12-oz. container frozen
    whipped topping, thawed
Optional: colored sugar

Prepare cake mix as directed for a 2-layer cake; set aside. Line two, 9" round cake pans with wax paper; pour in prepared cake mix. Bake according to package directions. Cool in pans. Poke holes in top of cake layers with a fork; set aside. Mix cherry gelatin with one cup boiling water. Carefully pour gelatin over one layer; set aside. Mix lime gelatin with remaining water; pour over second layer. Chill layers until completely set. Turn out first layer onto a serving plate; remove wax paper. Spread with whipped topping. Place second layer on top of first; remove wax paper. Continue to spread whipped topping over cake until covered. Sprinkle with colored sugar, if desired. Serves 12.

Make your own colored sugar…it's simple! Shake together 1/2 cup sugar and 5 to 7 drops food coloring in a small jar. Spread sugar on a baking sheet to dry.

Chocolate-Caramel Crispy Bars

Janet Graddy
Lake City, FL

Caramel, peanut butter and chocolate...all our very favorite flavors!

14-oz. pkg. caramels,
   unwrapped
3/4 c. creamy peanut butter,
   divided
1/4 c. water

1 c. butter, softened
1 c. semi-sweet chocolate chips
4 c. crispy rice cereal
1 c. peanuts

Place caramels, 1/2 cup peanut butter and water in a microwave-safe bowl; melt in microwave on medium-high setting. Stir until smooth. Spread in a greased 13"x9" baking pan; set aside. Place butter, chocolate chips and remaining peanut butter in a microwave-safe bowl; heat on medium-high setting until melted. Stir in cereal and nuts; spread over caramel mixture. Refrigerate until set; cut into bars. Makes about 2-1/2 dozen.

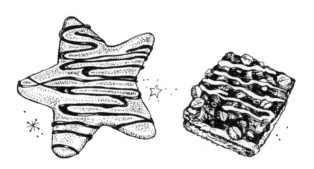

Any cookie is even yummier when drizzled with
chocolate! Place 1/3 cup chocolate chips in a small
plastic zipping bag and microwave for 45 to
60 seconds. Knead bag until chocolate is smooth,
then snip off a tiny corner and squeeze. Try white
chocolate chips for a different look.

Raspberry Crumb Bars

Wendy Lee Paffenroth
Pine Island, NY

Cut into dainty squares...just right to serve with a cup of tea.

1 c. butter, softened
1 t. vanilla extract
1/2 c. brown sugar, packed
1/4 c. sugar
2 c. all-purpose flour
1/8 t. salt

12-oz. pkg. chocolate chips,
  divided
14-oz. can sweetened
  condensed milk
1/2 c. raspberry jam

Combine butter, vanilla, sugars, flour and salt in a large mixing bowl.
Press 1-1/4 cups of mixture into the bottom of a lightly greased
13"x9" baking pan. Set remaining crumbs aside. Bake at 350 degrees
for 10 minutes; remove from oven. Combine one cup chocolate chips
with condensed milk in a small saucepan; melt over low heat until
smooth. Spread over crust. Sprinkle reserved crumbs over chocolate
mixture. Drop jam by teaspoonfuls over crumbs; sprinkle remaining
chocolate chips on top of jam. Bake at 350 degrees for an additional
30 minutes. Remove to a wire rack; let cool one hour. Cut into bars.
Makes about 2 dozen.

Corral those loose spools
of ribbon...just place
them on an upright paper
towel holder!

White Chocolate Chippers

Renae Scheiderer
Beallsville, OH

Stir in some chopped macadamia nuts for an extra-special treat.

1 c. butter, softened
2 c. sugar
2 eggs
2 t. vanilla extract
2 c. all-purpose flour

3/4 c. baking cocoa
1 t. baking soda
1/2 t. salt
10-oz. pkg. white chocolate
    chips

Blend butter and sugar together in a large bowl until creamy. Add eggs and vanilla; blend until light and fluffy. Set aside. Stir together flour, cocoa, baking soda and salt; gradually stir into butter mixture. Fold in chocolate chips. Drop by teaspoonfuls onto ungreased baking sheets. Bake at 350 degrees for 8 to 9 minutes. Let cool slightly; remove to wire racks to finish cooling. Makes 4-1/2 dozen.

A new paper paint pail makes a family-size gift container for cookies. Decorate with wrapping paper cut-outs attached with craft glue. Fill with cookies, set on a large sheet of colored cellophane and top with a bow...beautiful!

Sweets to SHARE

Mrs. Santa's Red Raspberry Ring

Patti Neuman
Fox Lake, WI

So pretty, refreshing and festive!

10-oz. pkg. frozen red
   raspberries, thawed
2 3-oz. pkgs. raspberry
   gelatin mix
2 c. boiling water

1 pt. vanilla ice cream
6-oz. can frozen pink lemonade
   concentrate, thawed
Optional: 1/4 c. chopped pecans

Drain raspberries, reserving the liquid; set aside. Dissolve gelatin in boiling water. Spoon ice cream into gelatin; stir until melted. Stir in reserved raspberry liquid and lemonade. Chill until partially set; add raspberries and pecans, if using. Turn into a 6-cup ring mold; chill until firm. Unmold onto a serving plate. Serves 8.

Snow Ice Cream

Tracy Day
Saint Louis, MO

A snow-day treat for the kids...use only freshly fallen snow.

1 c. milk
1 pasteurized egg, beaten
1/2 c. sugar

1 t. vanilla extract
1 t. cinnamon
8 c. clean, fresh snow

Blend first 5 ingredients together. Add snow until absorbed. Pack into a freezer-safe container and freeze until firm. Serves about 4.

Share the Christmas cards you receive from friends & family...simply tuck them among the branches of the Christmas tree.

Candy Cane Balls

Lisa Ludwig
Fort Wayne, IN

The perfect partner for a cup of hot cocoa.

1 c. butter, softened
1 c. sugar
1 egg
1/4 t. salt
2 t. vanilla extract

2-2/3 c. all-purpose flour
3/4 to 1 c. powdered sugar
3/4 to 1 c. peppermint candies,
   finely crushed

Blend together butter and sugar. Add egg, salt and vanilla; beat well. Stir in flour; chill for at least one hour. Mix together powdered sugar and crushed candies; set aside. Form dough into one-inch balls and place on lightly greased baking sheets. Bake at 375 degrees for 7 to 10 minutes. Immediately roll warm cookies in powdered sugar mixture. Makes 3 to 4 dozen.

Check a craft or cake decorating supply store for paste-style food coloring to create frosting in extra bright, deep colors.

Cinnamon Logs

Julie Dawson
Prospect Heights, IL

Christmas Eve morning was always special to my 4 siblings and me...that's when we exchanged small handmade gifts to each other. We took time to enjoy them before all of Santa's gifts came the next morning. Best of all, Mom let us eat Christmas cookies for breakfast!

1 c. butter, softened
1 t. almond extract
3 T. sugar

1 T. cinnamon
2 c. all-purpose flour
Garnish: powdered sugar

In a large bowl, blend together butter, almond extract, sugar and cinnamon until light and fluffy. Add flour and beat well. Chill for several hours until dough is firm enough to handle. Using palms of hands, shape teaspoonfuls of dough into one-inch logs. Arrange on ungreased baking sheets; bake at 300 degrees for about 20 minutes, or until golden. Cool on paper towels; sprinkle generously with powdered sugar. Makes 4 to 5 dozen.

Wonderful vintage holiday cookie tins can be found at tag sales...just pop in a tissue paper lining and they're ready to fill with baked goodies.

Dorothy's Cream Puff Cake

Dorothy Lo
Cleveland, OH

This dessert is very easy to make. It's so light too...just right after a holiday dinner!

1/2 c. butter
1 c. water
1 c. all-purpose flour
4 eggs

16-oz. container frozen
   whipped topping
Garnish: 1.55-oz. chocolate bar,
   grated into curls

Melt butter with water in a saucepan over medium heat. Remove from heat; stir in flour until dough forms into a ball. Add eggs one at a time, mixing by hand after each one until smooth. Spread dough to fill a lightly greased baking sheet. Bake at 325 degrees until golden; let cool. Spread Lemon Filling over crust; top with whipped topping. Sprinkle chocolate curls over topping. Makes 10 to 12 servings.

Lemon Filling:

8-oz. pkg. cream cheese,
   softened
3 c. milk

2 5-oz. pkgs. instant lemon
   pudding mix

Blend ingredients together until thick.

As many mince pies as you taste at Christmas,
so many happy years will you have.
-Old English Saying

Sweets to SHARE

Date-Nut-Cherry Fruitcake

Charlotte Page
Jay, ME

This recipe will make 4 gift-size mini loaves.

1-1/2 c. all-purpose flour
1-1/2 c. sugar
1 t. baking powder
1 t. salt
16-oz. pkg. chopped dates

16-oz. pkg. chopped walnuts
16-oz. jar maraschino cherries,
   drained
5 eggs, beaten
1 t. vanilla extract

Combine flour, sugar, baking powder and salt; stir in dates, walnuts and cherries. Set aside. Beat eggs and vanilla together; add to flour mixture. Pour into 2 greased 9"x5" loaf pans; bake at 325 degrees for one hour. Makes 2 fruitcakes.

No mantel for hanging stockings?
Mount Shaker pegs on a wooden board, one
for each member of the family!

Cranberry-Apple Pie

Nichole Martelli
Alvin, TX

Tasty apples and cranberries baked in a gingersnap crust...mmm!

20 gingersnaps
1-1/2 t. margarine
2 apples, cored, peeled
   and sliced
1 c. cranberries
5 T. brown sugar, packed

1/4 t. vanilla extract
1/4 t. cinnamon
1 t. sugar
Optional: frozen whipped
   topping, thawed

Place gingersnaps and margarine in a food processor or blender; process until ground. Press into an ungreased 8" pie plate. Bake at 375 degrees for 5 to 8 minutes; set aside to cool. Coarsely chop apples in food processor or blender. Add cranberries, brown sugar, vanilla and cinnamon; pulse just until mixed. Spoon apple mixture into another 8" pie plate lightly sprayed with non-stick vegetable spray; sprinkle sugar over top. Bake at 375 degrees for 35 minutes, or until apples are tender. Remove from oven; pour into cooled crust. Serve warm, garnished with whipped topping if desired. Serves 8.

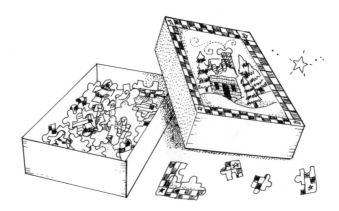

Lay out a Christmas-themed jigsaw puzzle on a table near the fireplace...holiday visitors will enjoy fitting a few pieces into place as they relax.

Espresso Biscotti

Stacie Mickley
Gooseberry Patch

Crunchy coffee dippers! Make them even better...stir some white chocolate chips into the dough, then drizzle finished cookies with melted dark chocolate.

3 T. coffee beans
2 T. coffee-flavored liqueur
   or double-strength
   brewed coffee
1/2 c. butter, softened
3/4 c. sugar

2 eggs
2 c. plus 2 T. all-purpose flour
1-1/2 t. baking powder
1/4 t. salt
2/3 c. slivered almonds, toasted

Grind coffee beans to a fine powder. Place in a small microwave-safe bowl; add liqueur or brewed coffee and heat on high setting for 10 to 15 seconds to steep. Set aside. Blend butter and sugar until light and fluffy; whisk in eggs and coffee bean mixture. Sift together flour, baking powder and salt; add to butter mixture, blending well. Fold in nuts. Divide dough in half. On a greased baking sheet, pat dough out into two, 13-inch by 1-1/2 inch by 1/2-inch rectangles, spacing them about 2 inches apart. Bake at 325 degrees for 20 to 25 minutes, or until golden. Remove to a wire rack; let cool for 5 minutes. Place on a cutting board; using a serrated knife, slice 1/2-inch thick diagonally at a 45-degree angle. Place slices upright on baking sheet 1/2 inch apart and return to oven for 10 minutes longer, until slightly dried. Let cool on rack. Store in a tightly covered container. Makes 2 dozen.

Slip Christmas cards into a vintage napkin holder as they arrive in your mailbox...share greetings from friends and relatives over dinner each day.

Mocha Shortbread

Carrie O'Shea
Marina Del Ray, CA

Delicious! Wrap up with a pound of gourmet coffee
as a gift for a coffee lover.

1-1/2 c. all-purpose flour
2 T. baking cocoa
4 t. instant coffee granules
1 t. vanilla extract

3/4 c. butter, softened
1/2 c. plus 2 t. sugar, divided
1/4 t. salt

Combine flour and cocoa in a large bowl; set aside. Stir together coffee and vanilla in another large bowl until coffee is dissolved. Add butter, 1/2 cup sugar and salt; mix well. Add flour mixture and stir just until blended. Press dough into an ungreased 9" round tart pan with removable bottom or 9" round cake pan. Bake at 300 degrees for 55 to 60 minutes, or until firm. Sprinkle with remaining sugar. Let cool in pan on wire rack for 5 to 10 minutes; cut into wedges. Makes 16.

Host a gift wrapping party! Gather up giftwrap, scissors and tape, play cheerful Christmas music and set out a plate of cookies for nibbling. With everyone helping each other, you'll be done in a snap!

Cider Mulling Spice Mix

Mary Wilson
Lansdale, PA

A cup of hot spiced cider really chases away the chills!

1 c. brown sugar, packed	1 t. ground cloves
2 t. cinnamon	1 t. allspice
1 t. orange zest	1/2 t. nutmeg
1 t. lemon zest	

Combine all ingredients in a food processor or blender. Pulse until zest is finely ground and ingredients are well mixed. Place in an airtight container; attach gift tag with instructions.

Instructions:

Combine one to 2 teaspoons spice mix with one cup cider in a small saucepan. Heat over medium-high heat until boiling; reduce heat and simmer for 5 minutes. Pour into mug. Makes about 24 servings.

Wrap up a container of Cider Mulling Spice Mix in a holiday napkin. Tie on a bow and a pair of cinnamon sticks for stirring...oh-so festive!

Christmas PANTRY

Minty Hot Chocolate Mix

Kaylene Duncan
Churubusco, IN

Attach a little bag of extra butter mints for nibbling.

2 c. chocolate malted milk
    powder, divided
1 c. butter mints

3 c. powdered milk
1-1/2 c. hot chocolate mix

Combine one cup malted milk powder and butter mints in a blender; process until smooth. Pour into a large mixing bowl. Add remaining ingredients and mix well. Place in an airtight container; attach gift tag with instructions.

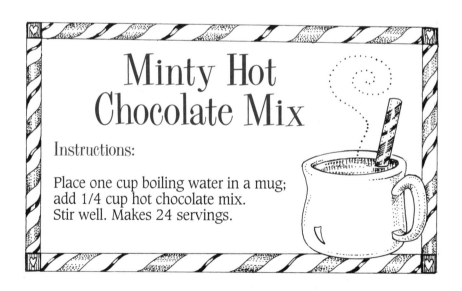

Minty Hot Chocolate Mix

Instructions:

Place one cup boiling water in a mug; add 1/4 cup hot chocolate mix. Stir well. Makes 24 servings.

Oh! the snow, the beautiful snow,
Filling the sky and earth below.
-J.W. Watson

Multi-Grain Pancake Mix

Jen Lindholm
Winona, MN

Nestle the pancake mix and a bottle of fruit-flavored syrup in a basket...perfect for breakfast lovers!

1/2 c. long-cooking oats, uncooked
2 c. all-purpose flour
1/2 c. whole-wheat flour
1/2 c. cornmeal
1/4 c. wheat bran

1/4 c. wheat germ, toasted
1/4 c. sugar
2 t. baking powder
1 t. baking soda
1-1/2 t. salt

Process oats in a food processor until smooth. Add remaining ingredients; continue to process until mix is smooth. Place mix in an airtight container; attach gift tag with instructions.

Instructions:

Keep pancake mix refrigerated until used. Combine one cup buttermilk, 3 tablespoons oil and 2 beaten egg whites; stir well. Add 1-1/2 cups pancake mix and stir until smooth. Spoon about 1/4 cup batter onto a lightly greased griddle over medium-high heat. Turn pancakes over when covered with bubbles and edges look done; cook other side. Makes about ten, 4-inch pancakes.

Dress up a plain paper bag for gift giving. Stamp all over with a holly leaf rubber stamp. Fold over the top, punch 2 holes and run a ribbon through to tie in a bow...done!

Ginger & Spice Muffin Mix

Marlene Burns
Swisher, IA

Sugar & spice and everything nice...that's what these muffins are made of!

1-3/4 c. all-purpose flour	1 t. cinnamon
1/2 c. sugar	1/2 t. nutmeg
1 T. baking powder	1/4 t. ground ginger
1/2 t. baking soda	1/4 t. ground cloves
1/2 t. salt	

Combine all ingredients in a large bowl; stir well. Place mix in an airtight container; attach gift tag with instructions.

Instructions:

Combine muffin mix, 1/4 cup melted butter, one egg, one teaspoon vanilla extract and one cup milk. Do not overmix; batter should be thick. Fill lightly greased muffin cups 2/3 full. Bake at 400 degrees for 15 minutes. Makes one dozen.

Check other chapters of this book for more yummy food gift ideas. How about a goodie bag of Golden North Pole Nuggets (p. 96) or a crock of Jalapeño Cheese Spread (p. 78) with a basket of crackers?

"I Love You" Soup in a Jar

Kerri Baer
Bothell, WA

Spell out a special greeting on the gift tag with extra alphabet macaroni!

1/2 c. dried split peas
1/3 c. beef bouillon granules
1/4 c. pearled barley
1/2 c. dried lentils
1/4 c. dried, minced onion
2 t. Italian salad dressing mix

1/2 c. long-cooking rice, uncooked
2 to 3 bay leaves
1/2 c. alphabet macaroni, uncooked

In a 1-1/2 pint, wide-mouth jar, layer all ingredients except alphabet macaroni. Place macaroni in a decorative bag; attach to jar along with gift tag with instructions.

Instructions:

Detach macaroni from jar and set aside. Brown one pound ground beef over medium heat in a large soup pot; drain. Add two, 14-1/2 ounce cans diced tomatoes, 6-ounce can tomato paste, 12 cups water and soup mix. Bring to a boil; reduce heat and simmer 45 minutes to one hour. Stir in macaroni; cover and simmer for an additional 15 minutes, until macaroni is tender. Discard bay leaves. Makes 10 to 12 servings.

Paint a round lidded paper maché box white, then paint a snowman face on the lid. Add clear glitter for icy sparkle.

Painted Desert Chili in a Jar

Amy Conrad
Enid, OK

The painted desert effect comes from the rippled appearance, like sand art. Bring out the beautiful colors by spooning each ingredient around the edges of the jar, then filling in the center.

1/4 c. plus 2 T. dried parsley, divided
1/4 c. dried, minced garlic, divided
1/4 c. plus 2 T. taco seasoning mix, divided
2 T. dried, minced onion
2 T. ground cumin

2 T. paprika
2 T. white cornmeal
2 T. chili powder
1 c. dried pinto beans
1/4 c. dried navy beans
1/4 c. dried black beans
1 c. dried kidney beans

Layer ingredients in a one-quart, wide-mouth jar as follows: 1/4 cup parsley, 2 tablespoons garlic, 2 tablespoons taco seasoning, onion, 2 tablespoons taco seasoning, cumin, paprika, cornmeal, remaining taco seasoning, then remaining garlic, chili powder, remaining parsley, pinto beans, navy beans, black beans and kidney beans. Attach gift tag with instructions.

Instructions:

Brown 2 pounds ground beef in a 12-quart stock pot; drain. Add contents of jar, 3/4 cup chopped onion, four, 14-1/2 ounce cans diced tomatoes, 12-ounce can tomato paste, 1/2 cup cider vinegar, 1/2 cup packed brown sugar, 49-ounce can tomato juice and browned ground beef. Fill remainder of pot with water. Bring to a boil; reduce heat and let simmer for 2-1/2 to 3 hours. Add salt and pepper to taste. Serves 10 to 12.

Tuck a jar of hearty soup mix into a big basket alongside a stack of chunky pottery bowls...a tummy-warming gift for a snowy day!

Marion's Fabulous Fudge

Marion Sundberg
Yorba Linda, CA

*Just for fun, cut this tasty fudge into football shapes, wrap and give
to a football fan along with the latest sports magazine.*

14-oz. can sweetened
  condensed milk
1-1/2 c. white chocolate chips

1/2 c. butterscotch chips
1/2 c. peanut butter chips
1/2 c. milk chocolate chips

Combine all ingredients in a heavy saucepan over medium heat.
Stir continuously until chips are melted. Pour into a lightly greased
aluminum foil-lined 8"x8" baking pan. Cool. Turn fudge out of pan;
peel off foil. Cut into squares. Makes 1-1/2 dozen squares.

Chocolate Turtles

Jennifer Stricker
Sellersburg, IN

Mini treats for a candy dish.

60 tiny pretzel twists
60 round chocolate-covered
  caramel candies

60 pecan halves

Spread a single layer of pretzel twists on an ungreased baking sheet.
Place one caramel candy in the center of each pretzel. Bake at
325 degrees for 3 minutes, or until candies are soft. Remove from
oven; immediately press pecans into softened candies. Let cool for
several hours; pack in cellophane bags. Makes 5 dozen.

Chinese take-out
containers are just right for
packing gifts of candies,
cookies or snack mix.

Maple-Pecan Fudge

Dianna Likens
Gooseberry Patch

The most scrumptious fudge ever!

3 c. sugar
5-oz. can evaporated milk
3/4 c. butter
12-oz. pkg. white
    chocolate chips

7-oz. jar marshmallow creme
1 t. vanilla extract
1 T. maple flavoring
1/2 to 1 c. pecans, chopped
    or halved

In a large saucepan, mix together sugar, evaporated milk and butter over medium heat, stirring constantly. Bring to a full rolling boil; continue stirring constantly at a full boil for 4 minutes. Remove from heat and stir in white chocolate chips and marshmallow creme; stir in vanilla and maple flavoring. Add chopped pecans, if using, or wait if using pecan halves. Pour warm fudge into a greased 11"x7" baking pan. If using pecan halves, press into top of fudge. Let set for several hours or overnight; cut into squares. Makes 2-1/2 dozen squares.

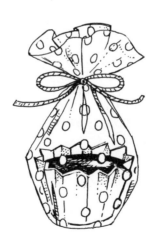

Mmm...super-size fudge cups! Just spoon warm fudge into foil muffin cups. Wrap individually in squares of colorful cellophane.

Christmas S'more Bars in a Jar

Cyndi Little
Whitsett, NC

*Such a fun jar mix to give and to bake! Cover the jar lid with a
4-inch circle of holiday fabric...tie with a raffia bow.*

1-1/2 c. graham cracker crumbs
1/3 c. brown sugar, packed
1-1/4 c. red and green candy-
    coated chocolates, divided

8 Christmas tree or
    snowman-shaped
    marshmallows

Place graham cracker crumbs in a one-quart, wide-mouth jar;
press down crumbs with a wooden tamper or the back of a spoon.
Add brown sugar on top of crumbs, gently pressing down. Pour
3/4 cup candy-coated chocolates over brown sugar. Arrange the
marshmallows inside jar, standing up and facing out; gently press
them against the glass without mashing. Pour remaining chocolates
behind marshmallows. Attach gift tag with instructions.

Instructions:

Empty contents of jar into a large bowl. Cut marshmallows into
small pieces; add to bowl. Stir until well blended. Combine 1/2 cup
melted butter and one teaspoon vanilla extract. Add butter mixture
to dry ingredients, mixing well. Pat into a greased 9"x9" baking pan;
bake at 350 degrees for 15 minutes. Cool and cut into bars.
Makes 9 to 12 bars.

Paint a wooden holiday
cut-out and hand-letter the
recipient's name for a gift
tag that doubles as a
tree ornament! Look for
fun shapes like mittens,
Santas and stars at a
craft store.

Christmas
PANTRY

Yummy Cookies in a Jar

Jennifer Burke
Deltona, FL

I give this cookie mix every year as gifts...everyone loves it!

1/2 c. white chocolate chips
1/2 c. crispy rice cereal
1-1/2 c. all-purpose flour
1 t. baking soda
1/2 c. brown sugar, packed

1/2 c. semi-sweet chocolate chips
1/2 c. long-cooking oats, uncooked
1/2 c. sugar

Layer all ingredients in given order in a one-quart, wide-mouth jar. Attach gift tag with instructions.

Instructions:

Blend together 1/2 cup margarine, one egg and one tablespoon vanilla extract. Add cookie mix and stir until well blended. Drop by tablespoonfuls onto a lightly greased baking sheet. Bake at 350 degrees for 10 minutes. Makes 2 to 2-1/2 dozen.

Make a frosty polka-dotted jar for your cookie mix! Create a dot pattern on a plain glass jar by pressing on round paper stickers. Brush on glass etching paint, following package directions. When paint sets, peel off stickers to reveal the design.

Grandma Doris's Caramels

*Doris Wilson
Denver, IA*

*My favorite holiday treat to give to friends and neighbors...I've been
making these caramels for 30 years! My grandchildren and I love
to make homemade tags for them using old cards and papers
decorated with sparkly paints...the possibilities are endless!*

2 c. sugar
16-oz. bottle light corn syrup
1/2 c. plus 3 T. butter

1/8 t. salt
2 c. evaporated milk

Mix together all ingredients except evaporated milk in a heavy
saucepan. Bring to a boil over medium heat, stirring occasionally.
Cook for 10 minutes. Gradually add evaporated milk, stirring well.
Bring mixture back to a boil and cook until it reaches the softball
stage, 234 to 243 degrees on a candy thermometer. Pour into a
greased 13"x9" baking pan. Cool and cut into squares; wrap in wax
paper. Store in a cool place. Makes 9 to 10 dozen.

Make your own tiny Christmas village for the mantel.
Paint wooden mini birdhouses from a craft store to
create houses, barns, a church...whatever you like!
Trim with drifts of white snow paint and arrange on a
landscape of fluffy cotton batting.

Christmas
PANTRY

Victorian Sugarplums

Marlene Darnell
Newport Beach, CA

*Dip sugarplums into melted white chocolate and
sprinkle with colored sugar...so pretty in a candy box!*

1 c. blanched almonds
3/4 c. chopped walnuts
3/4 c. raisins
3/4 c. dried apricots

3/4 c. chopped dates
1/4 c. orange juice
Garnish: sparkling sugar

Combine nuts and fruit in a blender or food processor; process until
mixture resembles coarse meal. Add orange juice; blend until mixture
holds together. Form into one-inch balls and roll in sugar; place
sugarplums in decorative paper candy cups. Store in an airtight
container in the refrigerator. Makes 2 to 2-1/2 dozen.

Give a giant peppermint stick filled with cookies! Stack
cookies in a clear plastic mailing tube, then spiral red
craft tape around the tube...oh-so easy!

Angie's Chai Tea Mix

*Angie Reedy
Mackinaw, IL*

*Present this tea mix along with a fabric-covered journal
for jotting down thoughts in quiet moments...so relaxing!*

2-1/2 c. powdered sugar
1 c. instant tea mix
1 c. powdered milk
1 c. powdered non-dairy creamer
1/2 c. vanilla-flavored powdered
   non-dairy creamer

1-1/2 t. pumpkin pie spice
1/2 t. ground ginger
1/4 t. ground cloves
1/2 t. cinnamon
1/2 t. cardamom

Mix all ingredients well; store in an airtight container. Attach gift tag
with instructions.

Chai Tea Mix

Instructions:

Add 1/3 cup tea mix to 1/2 cup
boiling water in a mug. Serves 6 to 9.

One sip of this will bathe the drooping spirits in
delight, beyond the bliss of dreams.
-John Milton

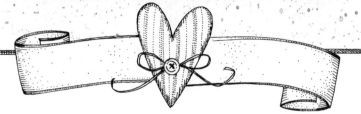

Ashley's Sugar & Spice Milk Bath

Ashley Printz
Ephrata, PA

One year, I knew that money would need to be stretched just a little further for the holidays. I decided to make homemade gifts for everyone. This milk bath was a HUGE hit and is still requested on friends' Christmas lists!

1 c. powdered milk	1/2 t. ground ginger
1/2 c. baking soda	1/4 t. ground cloves
2 T. sugar	6 to 8 drops cinnamon or
1 t. cinnamon	vanilla essential oil

Mix all ingredients together until well blended. Place in a large jar or divide into several cellophane bags and tie with raffia or homespun. Attach gift tags with instructions. Makes about 1-1/2 cups.

Instructions:

Scoop out 1/4 cup bath mix and dissolve under warm running water…soak and enjoy!

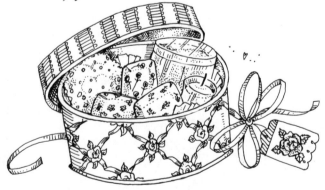

Give homemade bath mixes with a pampering bath set!
Cover a hatbox in vintage wallpaper, then fill with
shredded tissue. Nestle a jar of bath mix, scented soaps
and a soft bath sponge inside. Sweet!

Handmade & HEARTFELT

Lilac Garden Bubble Bath

Laura Lett
Gooseberry Patch

Perfect for pampering!

4 c. distilled water
1 c. unscented baby shampoo

6 T. glycerin
5 drops lilac essential oil

Mix all ingredients together; store in an airtight container. Attach gift tag. Makes about 5 cups.

Caribbean Bath Salt Crystals

Regina Wickline
Pebble Beach, CA

Tie on a color postcard of a tropical scene as a fun gift tag!

4 c. Epsom salt
6 to 8 drops blue and green
    food coloring

10 drops orange essential oil
10 drops lemongrass essential
    oil

Place Epsom salt in a large mixing bowl. Stir in food coloring, a few drops at a time, until desired tint is achieved. Slowly add essential oils. Pour into an airtight container; attach gift tag. Makes about 4 cups.

A serving tray is oh-so handy! Repaint a tag sale find or pick up a plain wooden tray from a craft store. Cut out pictures from Christmas cards and glue on with craft glue. Give the tray a protective coating of polyurethane finish.

205

Fruity Lip Gloss

Abby Bills
Orleans, NE

Great stocking stuffers that girls can make by themselves!
Look for mini plastic containers at art supply stores.

2 T. shortening   4 to 6 1/2-oz. lidded pots
1 T. fruit-flavored drink mix

Combine shortening and drink mix in a microwave-safe bowl;
mix well. Microwave on high setting for about 30 seconds, or until
shortening mix is melted. Spoon into pots and secure lids. Refrigerate
for 20 to 30 minutes, until firm. Makes 4 to 6 pots.

Turn a small notebook into a charming purse planner
for Mom...simply glue on pretty papers, stickers and
other scrapbooking embellishments! Add a pocket
calendar and an address book
to create a ribbon-tied set.

Handmade & HEARTFELT

Candy Cane Bath Salts

Wendy Savage
Rocklin, CA

Tie the instructions, a small scoop and several mini candy canes onto each jar with a red ribbon.

4 c. Epsom salt, divided
1 c. sea salt, divided
8 to 12 drops peppermint
   essential oil

4 to 6 drops red food coloring
4 1/2-pint jars and lids

Place one cup Epsom salt and 1/4 cup sea salt in a plastic zipping bag. Add 2 to 3 drops peppermint oil; set aside. Place remaining salts, peppermint oil and food coloring in a small mixing bowl; mix well. Layer red and white salts in four, 1/2-pint jars, tilting jars as you fill them. Seal with lids and attach gift tags with instructions. Makes 4 jars.

Candy Cane Bath Salts

Instructions:
Add a scoop or 2 of bath salts to running water.

Novelty shoestrings make an unexpected, fun substitute for ribbons when wrapping gifts!

Kitty Cat Treats

Marilyn Miller
Fort Washington, PA

Decorate the container with pompoms of brightly colored yarn...they'll double as playthings for your favorite cat!

9-oz. can tuna, drained
1-1/2 c. whole-grain
   bread crumbs
1/2 t. brewer's yeast

1-1/2 t. oil
1 egg, beaten
1 t. garlic powder

Place tuna in a small bowl and flake with a fork; mix in remaining ingredients. Drop by 1/4 teaspoonfuls onto a greased baking sheet. Bake at 350 degrees for 8 minutes. Cool to room temperature and refrigerate in an airtight container. Makes 7 to 8 dozen.

Wrap a long string of sparkly glass craft beads around
a glass votive, securing each end with
craft glue. Drop in a votive candle...the beads
will glow in the candlelight!

Handmade &
HEARTFELT

Homemade Doggie Bones

Shirl Kriekel
Brookfield, IL

My best (doggie) friends are so excited when I bake them these special cookies...with a secret ingredient, love!

1 c. whole-wheat flour
1 c. cornmeal
1 c. wheat germ
1/2 c. soy flour
1/2 c. powdered milk

2 T. brewer's yeast
1/2 c. oil
2 eggs
1 T. honey
3/4 c. water

Combine first 6 ingredients in a large bowl. Add oil and blend until mixture resembles coarse meal. Beat in eggs, honey and enough water to form a stiff dough. Work with hands until pliable. Roll dough out to 1/2-inch thick; cut with bone-shaped cookie cutters. Arrange on a lightly greased baking sheet. Bake at 375 degrees for 30 minutes. Makes 2 to 2-1/2 dozen.

Wrap up Grandmother's big yellowware mixing bowl along with her prized cookie recipe for a daughter who's learning to bake. She'll love it!

Christmas Scent Mix

Melissa Dunlap
Indiana, PA

Each Christmas I make homemade goodies for special friends and family members. This delicious-smelling scent mix was created for a calorie-counting friend so she could keep her girlish figure!

1 whole lemon
1 whole orange
3 4-inch cinnamon sticks

6 bay leaves
1/2 c. whole cloves

Combine all ingredients and place in a decorative plastic bag. Attach gift tag with instructions. Makes one bag.

Instructions:

Cut unpeeled lemon and orange into quarters. Combine fruit, spices and 2 quarts water in a saucepan. Bring to a boil; reduce heat and simmer as long as desired, continuing to add water as needed. Cover any leftover mixture; may be refrigerated for several days and reused.

Decorate a pocket-size candy tin as a delightful container for a gift of jewelry. Paint it with craft spray paint and découpage a vintage cut-out on the lid. It'll be treasured like an extra little gift.

Magic Reindeer Food

Kristi Boyle
Easton, MD

A sweet Christmas Eve tradition to share with a small friend.

1/2 c. oatmeal
1/4 c. sugar

red and green candy sprinkles

Mix all ingredients together and place in a plastic zipping bag.
Tie with ribbon and attach a gift tag with the following poem.
Makes one bag.

Sprinkle on your lawn at night,
The moon will make it sparkle bright.
As Santa's reindeer fly and roam,
This sweet treat will guide them to
your home.

Make gift shopping twice as easy…when you
find a useful kitchen utensil or handy household item
for yourself, just buy 2! Tuck away the
extras in a big box for future gift-giving.

Bubble Fun Bath Jelly

Teri Cochran
Talking Rock, GA

Attach a heart-shaped tablespoon to the jar for scooping.

1 env. unflavored gelatin
3/4 c. boiling water
1/2 c. clear liquid soap

5 to 8 drops favorite-fragrance
    essential oil
1 drop food coloring

Dissolve gelatin in boiling water. Add remaining ingredients and stir gently. Pour into a jar and seal with lid; refrigerate for about 4 hours, or until set. Attach gift tag with instructions. Makes 1-1/4 cups.

Instructions:

Scoop out one to 2 tablespoons bath jelly and dissolve under warm running water.

A winter snow kit for the car is a gift Dad will appreciate! Pack a duffle bag with a snow scraper, a warm pair of new gloves, a folding snow shovel and a flashlight. Tie on a big tag that says "Thinking warm thoughts of you!"

Aphrodite's Bath Soak

Sara Buster
Webster Groves, MO

A vintage cut-glass cruet would make a beautiful container
for this skin-softening soak that's fit for a queen.

1 c. sesame oil
1 c. unscented liquid
  soap

4 drops ylang-ylang essential oil
3 drops neroli essential oil
2 drops bergamot essential oil

Combine all ingredients; pour into a one-pint jar and seal with lid.
Attach gift tag with instructions. Makes 2 cups.

Instructions:

Shake well. Add one to 2 tablespoons to warm water.

Dresser drawer sachets are a quick & easy gift!
Sew tiny pillows of homespun fabric or
wide ribbon, place a bit of fragrant potpourri
inside and stitch closed.

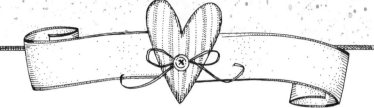

Raspberry-Oatmeal Hand Cream

Dana Cunningham
Lafayette, LA

Soothes hands roughened by winter.

1/2 c. distilled water
1/8 t. borax
1 T. beeswax, chopped
1/3 c. sweet almond oil
1 T. lanolin

1 t. coconut oil
15 drops raspberry essential oil
5 drops oatmeal, milk & honey
  essential oil

Combine water and borax in a heavy saucepan over low heat; stir until borax dissolves. Set aside. In a small saucepan over low heat, melt beeswax, almond oil and lanolin together, stirring until well blended. Remove from heat. Slowly, one teaspoon at a time, add borax mixture, stirring constantly. Continue stirring until a thick white cream forms; cool to room temperature. Add oils, blending well. Pour into a decorative jar and seal. Attach gift tag. Makes one jar.

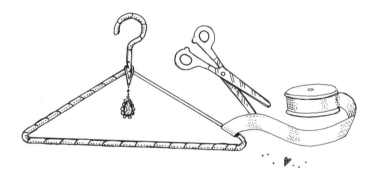

Make a ribbon-covered clothes hanger or 2 for an elegant gift. Wrap a 6-yard length of narrow velvet ribbon around a sturdy wire hanger, starting and ending at the hook. Tack end in place and add a tiny charm or silk flower...done!

Handmade & HEARTFELT

Rose Garden Hand Lotion

Beth Kramer
Port Saint Lucie, FL

Add just a drop of red food coloring for rosy pink lotion.

2/3 c. rosewater

1/3 c. glycerin

Combine rosewater and glycerin in a decorative bottle. Seal; shake well. Attach gift tag. Makes one bottle.

Sparkly Body Glitter

Teri Cochran
Talking Rock, GA

A fun stocking stuffer for a special girl.

3 T. unmedicated aloe vera gel
1/2 t. very fine glitter

Optional: 1 drop favorite-fragrance essential oil

Stir together aloe vera gel and glitter. Add essential oil, if desired. Stir until blended; place in a small airtight container. Makes one container.

The holly's up, the house is all bright.
The tree is ready, The candles alight.
Rejoice and be glad, all children tonight!
-Carl Cornelius

Nifty Gifty CARDS & TAGS

Just copy, cut & attach to all your gifts and gift mixes.

Send a note to loved ones along with a photograph or fill in information for a holiday party invitation!

There's no place like

HOME

for the HOLIDAYS

To:

From:

1. Copy 2. Color 3. Cut Out!

May peace be your gift at CHRISTMAS & Your Blessing all year through. —author unknown

Give a gift from the ♡

Be Merry!

JINGLE BELLS

Let it Snow!

PEACE,

Have a Merry Christmas

JOY

Write a recipe on the back!

HAPPY HOLIDAYS!

From the kitchen of:

....

Use a hole punch and colored ribbon to decorate.

Glue to colored cardstock to make a greeting card!

Warm Wishes

Index

Index

Index

We've cooked up a whole collection of Gooseberry Patch® books!

Have a taste for more? Call us toll-free at
1-800-854-6673
We'll send you our latest catalog filled with kitchenware, candles, handmade quilts, gourmet goodies, enamelware, bowls, bubble night lights and our very own line of cookbooks, calendars and organizers!

Phone us:
1·800·854·6673

Fax us:
1·740·363·7225

Visit our website:
www.gooseberrypatch.com

Send us your favorite recipe!

and the memory that makes it special for you! If we select your recipe for a brand new **Gooseberry Patch** cookbook, your name will appear right along with it...and you'll receive a FREE copy of the book! Mail to:

Gooseberry Patch
Attn: Book Dept.
P.O. Box 190
Delaware, OH 43015

*Please include the number of servings and all other necessary information!

U.S. to Canadian recipe equivalents

Volume Measurements

1/4 teaspoon	1 mL
1/2 teaspoon	2 mL
1 teaspoon	5 mL
1 tablespoon = 3 teaspoons	15 mL
2 tablespoons = 1 fluid ounce	30 mL
1/4 cup	60 mL
1/3 cup	75 mL
1/2 cup = 4 fluid ounces	125 mL
1 cup = 8 fluid ounces	250 mL
2 cups = 1 pint =16 fluid ounces	500 mL
4 cups = 1 quart	1 L

Weights

1 ounce	30 g
4 ounces	120 g
8 ounces	225 g
16 ounces = 1 pound	450 g

Oven Temperatures

300° F	150° C
325° F	160° C
350° F	180° C
375° F	190° C
400° F	200° C
450° F	230° C

Baking Pan Sizes

Square

8x8x2 inches	2 L = 20x20x5 cm
9x9x2 inches	2.5 L = 23x23x5 cm

Rectangular

13x9x2 inches	3.5 L = 33x23x5 cm

Loaf

9x5x3 inches	2 L = 23x13x7 cm

Round

8x1-1/2 inches	1.2 L = 20x4 cm
9x1-1/2 inches	1.5 L = 23x4 cm